NO FEAR SHAKESPEARE

NO FEAR SHAKESPEARE

NO FEAR SHAKESPEARE

AS YOU LIKE IT

SPARK
NOTES

The original text and translation for this edition was prepared by John Crowther.

Spark Publishing
A Division of Barnes & Noble Booksellers, Inc.
120 Fifth Avenue
New York, NY 10011
www.sparknotes.com

ISBN 978-1-4114-0104-4

Library of Congress Cataloging-in-Publication Data

Shakespeare, William, 1564–1616.
  As you like it / [edited by John Crowther].
    p. cm.—(No fear Shakespeare)
ISBN-13: 978-1-4114-0104-4
ISBN-10: 1-4114-0104-2
  1. Fathers and daughters—Drama. 2. Exiles—Drama. I. Crowther, John (John C.)
  II. Title.
PR2803.A2C76 2004
822.3'3—dc22

                        2004009850

Manufactured in Canada

40 39 38 37 36 35 34 33

There's matter in these sighs, these profound heaves.
You must translate: 'tis fit we understand them.

(Hamlet, 4.1.1–2)

FEAR NOT.

Have you ever found yourself looking at a Shakespeare play, then down at the footnotes, then back at the play, and still not understanding? You know what the individual words mean, but they don't add up. SparkNotes' *No Fear Shakespeare* will help you break through all that. Put the pieces together with our easy-to-read translations. Soon you'll be reading Shakespeare's own words fearlessly—and actually enjoying it.

No Fear Shakespeare puts Shakespeare's language side-by-side with a facing-page translation into modern English—the kind of English people actually speak today. When Shakespeare's words make your head spin, our translation will help you sort out what's happening, who's saying what, and why.

AS YOU LIKE IT

CHARACTERS

Rosalind—The heroine of the play. Rosalind is the daughter of the exiled Duke Senior and the constant companion of her cousin Celia. She is independent-minded, strong-willed, good-hearted, and terribly clever. Rather than slink off into defeated exile, Rosalind resourcefully uses her trip to the Forest of Arden as an opportunity to take control of her own destiny. When she disguises herself as Ganymede, a handsome young man, and offers herself as a tutor in the ways of love to her beloved Orlando, Rosalind's talents and charms are on full display. Rosalind teaches those around her to think, feel, and love better than they have previously, and ensures that the courtiers returning from Arden are gentler than when they fled to it.

Orlando—The youngest son of Sir Rowland de Bois and younger brother of Oliver. Orlando is a handsome young man who, under his brother's neglectful care, has languished without a gentleman's education or training. Regardless, he considers himself to have great potential, and his victorious battle with Charles proves him right. Orlando cares for the aging Adam in the Forest of Arden and later risks his life to save Oliver from a hungry lioness, proving himself a proper gentleman and fitting mate for Rosalind.

Duke Senior—The father of Rosalind and the rightful ruler of the dukedom in which the play is set. Having been banished by his usurping brother, Frederick, Duke Senior now lives in exile in the Forest of Arden with a number of loyal men, including Lord Amiens and Jaques. Far from resenting his banishment, Duke Senior celebrates his life in the forest and his freedom from the rivalries and corruption of the court.

Content in the forest, where he claims to learn as much from stones and brooks as he would in a church or library, Duke Senior demonstrates himself to be a kind and fair-minded ruler.

Jaques—A faithful lord who accompanies Duke Senior into exile in the Forest of Arden. Jaques is an example of a stock figure in Elizabethan comedy, the man possessed of a hopelessly melancholy disposition. Jaques stands on the sidelines of life, watching and judging the actions of the other characters without ever fully participating in the action around him. Jaques alone refuses to follow Duke Senior and the other courtiers back to court, and instead resolves to assume a solitary and contemplative life in a monastery.

Celia—The daughter of Duke Frederick and Rosalind's dearest friend. Celia's devotion to Rosalind is unmatched, as evidenced by her decision to follow her cousin into exile. To make the trip, Celia assumes the disguise of a simple shepherdess and calls herself Aliena. As we see from her extreme love of Rosalind and her immediate devotion to Oliver, whom she marries at the end of the play, Celia possesses a loving heart, but is impetuous and prone to deep, almost excessive emotions.

Duke Frederick—The brother of Duke Senior and usurper of his throne. Duke Frederick's cruel nature and volatile temper are displayed when he banishes his niece, Rosalind, from court without reason. That Celia, his own daughter, cannot mitigate his unfounded anger demonstrates the intensity of the duke's hatefulness. Frederick mounts an army against his exiled brother but aborts his vengeful mission after he meets an old religious man on the road to the Forest of Arden.

Touchstone—A clown or jester in Duke Frederick's court who accompanies Rosalind and Celia in their flight to Arden. Although it is Touchstone's job, as a professional fool, to criticize the behavior and point out the folly of those around him, he does so in a very different style from Rosalind. Compared with his mistress, Touchstone is hilariously vulgar and unromantic, infusing almost every line he speaks with bawdy innuendo.

Oliver—The oldest son of Sir Rowland de Bois and sole inheritor of the de Bois estate. Oliver is a loveless young man who begrudges his brother, Orlando, a gentleman's education. He admits to hating Orlando without cause or reason, and goes to great lengths to ensure Orlando's downfall.

Silvius—A young shepherd desperately in love with the proud and disdainful Phoebe. Following the conventions of the love poetry of the time, Silvius prostrates himself before a woman who refuses to return his affections. In the end, however, he wins the object of his desire.

Phoebe—A young shepherdess who disdains the affections of Silvius. She falls in love with Ganymede, who is really Rosalind in disguise, but Rosalind tricks Phoebe into marrying Silvius.

Lord Amiens—A faithful lord who accompanies Duke Senior into exile in the Forest of Arden. Lord Amiens is jolly and loves to sing.

Charles—A professional wrestler in Duke Frederick's court. Charles demonstrates both his caring nature and his political savvy when he asks Oliver to intercede in his upcoming fight with Orlando: He does not want to injure the young man and thereby lose favor among the nobles who support him. Charles's concern for Orlando proves unwarranted when Orlando beats him senseless.

Adam—The ancient former servant of Sir Rowland de Bois. Having witnessed Orlando's hardships, Adam offers not only to accompany his young master into exile but to fund their journey with the whole of his modest life's savings. He is a model of loyalty and devoted service.

Sir Rowland de Bois—The father of Oliver and Orlando, friend of Duke Senior, and enemy of Duke Frederick. Upon Sir Rowland's death, the vast majority of his estate was handed over to Oliver according to the custom of primogeniture.

Corin—A shepherd. Corin attempts to counsel his friend Silvius in the ways of love, but Silvius refuses to listen.

Audrey—A simpleminded goatherd who agrees to marry Touchstone, despite the fact that she understands very little of what he says.

William—A young country boy in love with Audrey, and thus Touchstone's rival.

AS YOU LIKE IT

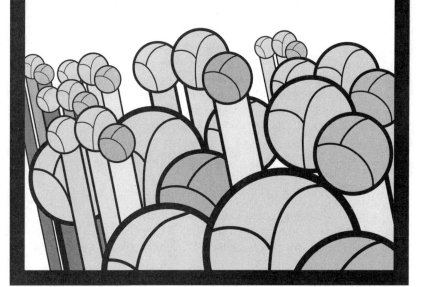

ACT ONE
SCENE 1

Enter ORLANDO *and* ADAM

ORLANDO

As I remember, Adam, it was upon this fashion
bequeathed me by will but poor a thousand crowns, and, as
thou sayest, charged my brother on his blessing to breed me
well. And there begins my sadness. My brother Jaques he
keeps at school, and report speaks goldenly of his profit. For
my part, he keeps me rustically at home or, to speak more
properly, stays me here at home unkept; for call you that
"keeping" for a gentleman of my birth that differs not from
the stalling of an ox? His horses are bred better, for, besides
that they are fair with their feeding, they are taught their
manage and, to that end, riders dearly hired. But I, his
brother, gain nothing under him but growth, for the which
his animals on his dunghills are as much bound to him as I.
Besides this nothing that he so plentifully gives me, the
something that nature gave me his countenance seems to
take from me. He lets me feed with his hinds, bars me the
place of a brother, and, as much as in him lies, mines my
gentility with my education. This is it, Adam, that grieves
me, and the spirit of my father, which I think is within me,
begins to mutiny against this servitude. I will no longer
endure it, though yet I know no wise remedy how to avoid
it.

Enter OLIVER

ADAM

Yonder comes my master, your brother.

ORLANDO

Go apart, Adam, and thou shalt hear how he will shake me up.

ACT ONE
SCENE 1

ORLANDO *and* ADAM *enter.*

ORLANDO

The actual reason is never made clear; the audience has happened upon a conversation already in progress.

I remember, Adam, that's exactly why my father only left me a thousand crowns in his will. And as you know, my father commanded my brother, Oliver, to make sure that I was brought up well—and that's where my sadness begins. Oliver keeps my brother Jaques away at school, and everyone says he's doing extremely well there. But he keeps me at home in the country—to be precise, he keeps me stuck at home but doesn't support me. I ask you, is this any way to treat a gentleman as nobly born as I am, to pen me in like an ox? His horses get treated better than I do—at least he feeds them and trains them properly, and spends a lot of money on trainers for them. All I've gained from his care is weight, which makes me as indebted to him as his animals on the manure pile are. He gives me plenty of nothing, and takes away everything else, letting me eat with his servants, refusing me what's owed me as his brother, and ruining my good birth with a poor education. This is what angers me, Adam. My father's temper and spirit, which I think I share, makes me want to mutiny against my brother's tyranny. I won't stand for it any longer, though I haven't yet figured out how to revolt.

OLIVER *enters.*

ADAM

Here comes my master, your brother.

ORLANDO

Go hide, Adam, and you'll hear how he abuses me.

OLIVER

25   Now, sir, what make you here?

ORLANDO

Nothing. I am not taught to make anything.

OLIVER

What mar you then, sir?

ORLANDO

Marry, sir, I am helping you to mar that which God made, a poor unworthy brother of yours, with idleness.

OLIVER

30   Marry, sir, be better employed, and be naught awhile.

ORLANDO

Shall I keep your hogs and eat husks with them? What prodigal portion have I spent that I should come to such penury?

OLIVER

Know you where you are, sir?

ORLANDO

35   O sir, very well: here in your orchard.

OLIVER

Know you before whom, sir?

ORLANDO

Ay, better than him I am before knows me. I know you are my eldest brother, and in the gentle condition of blood you should so know me. The courtesy of nations allows you my
40   better, in that you are the first-born, but the same tradition takes not away my blood, were there twenty brothers betwixt us. I have as much of my father in me as you, albeit, I confess, your coming before me is nearer to his reverence.

OLIVER

Oliver means "what are you doing here," but Orlando interprets "making" in its usual sense.

Hey, you! What are you making here?

ORLANDO

Nothing. I've never been taught how to make anything.

OLIVER

Well, then, what are you messing up?

ORLANDO

I'm helping *you* mess up one of God's creations—your poor, unworthy brother—by having him do nothing.

OLIVER

Indeed, sir, find something better to do and get lost for a while.

ORLANDO

Orlando alludes to the prodigal son, a figure from the Bible who leaves home, spends all his money, and returns to his father's house in poverty (Luke 15).

Should I tend your pigs and eat husks with them? When did I waste so much money that I ended up this poor?

OLIVER

Do you know where you are, sir?

ORLANDO

Yes, sir, very well—I'm here in your orchard.

OLIVER

Do you know whom you're talking to?

ORLANDO

Yes, better than you know me. I know you're my oldest brother, and deserve more respect. But we're in the same family, so you should acknowledge that I am a gentleman too. According to custom, as the first-born you are my superior. But it's not customary to treat me like I'm not even a gentleman, even if there were twenty brothers between you and me. I have as much of our father in me as you do, though I admit you're closer to him and matter more because you're older.

OLIVER

What, boy! *(strikes him)*

ORLANDO

45 Come, come, elder brother, you are too young in
this. *(seizes him)*

OLIVER

Wilt thou lay hands on me, villain?

ORLANDO

I am no villain. I am the youngest son of Sir Rowland de
Boys. He was my father, and he is thrice a villain that says
50 such a father begot villains. Wert thou not my brother, I
would not take this hand from thy throat till this other had
pulled out thy tongue for saying so. Thou hast railed on
thyself.

ADAM

Sweet masters, be patient. For your father's remembrance,
55 be at accord.

OLIVER

Let me go, I say.

ORLANDO

I will not till I please. You shall hear me. My father charged
you in his will to give me good education. You have trained
me like a peasant, obscuring and hiding from me all
60 gentlemanlike qualities. The spirit of my father grows
strong in me, and I will no longer endure it. Therefore allow
me such exercises as may become a gentleman, or give me
the poor allottery my father left me by testament. With that
I will go buy my fortunes.

OLIVER

65 And what wilt thou do—beg when that is spent? Well, sir,
get you in. I will not long be troubled with you. You shall
have some part of your will. I pray you leave me.

OLIVER

(hitting ORLANDO*)* What nerve!

ORLANDO

(grabbing hold of OLIVER*)* Come on, big brother; you don't know anything about fighting.

OLIVER

What, you dare put your hands on me, villain?

ORLANDO

I'm no villain. I'm the youngest son of Sir Rowland de Boys, and anyone who claims my father's sons are villains is a villain himself. If you weren't my brother, I'd leave this hand of mine on your neck until I'd pulled out your tongue for talking like this. You've only insulted yourself.

ADAM

Gentlemen, calm down. For the sake of your father's memory, make peace.

OLIVER

Let me go, I say.

ORLANDO

I won't until I'm ready. You will listen to me. My father instructed you in his will to give me a good education. But you've raised me as a peasant, hiding from me what I needed to become a gentleman. My father's spirit is growing in me, and I won't take this any longer. Either give me the freedom to act like someone of my own rank or give me my share of the inheritance, so that I can seek my fortune elsewhere.

OLIVER

And what are you going to do after you've spent your money? Beg? Well, sir, go inside. I'm not going to be bothered by you for long. You'll get some of what you want. Now please leave me alone.

ORLANDO
    I will no further offend you than becomes me for my good.

OLIVER
    Get you with him, you old dog.

ADAM

70   Is "old dog" my reward? Most true, I have lost my teeth in
    your service. God be with my old master. He would not
    have spoke such a word.

Exeunt ORLANDO *and* ADAM

OLIVER
    Is it even so? Begin you to grow upon me? I will physic your
    rankness and yet give no thousand crowns neither.—Holla,
75   Dennis!

Enter DENNIS

DENNIS
    Calls your Worship?

OLIVER
    Was not Charles, the duke's wrestler, here to speak with
    me?

DENNIS
    So please you, he is here at the door and importunes access
80   to you.

OLIVER
    Call him in.

Exit DENNIS

    'Twill be a good way, and tomorrow the wrestling is.

Enter CHARLES

ORLANDO

I won't bother you any more than necessary.

OLIVER

(to ADAM*)* And you get lost too, you old dog.

ADAM

Is that my reward—to be called "old dog?" Well, it's true, I've served this family so long I've gotten old and toothless, like a dog. God bless my old master. He would never have spoken to me like this.

ORLANDO *and* ADAM *exit.*

OLIVER

Is that how it's going to be? Are you starting to challenge me? I'll cure you of your insolence, and I'm not going to give you a thousand crowns, either!—Hey, Dennis!

DENNIS *enters.*

DENNIS

Did you call for me, your Worship?

OLIVER

Wasn't Charles, the duke's wrestler, here to speak with me?

DENNIS

Yes, sir, he's here at the door right now and asks to see you.

OLIVER

Call him in.

DENNIS *exits.*

I have a good plan. And tomorrow is the wrestling match.

CHARLES *enters.*

CHARLES
Good morrow to your Worship.

OLIVER
Good Monsieur Charles, what's the new news at the new
85   court?

CHARLES
There's no news at the court, sir, but the old news. That is,
the old duke is banished by his younger brother the new
duke, and three or four loving lords have put themselves
into voluntary exile with him, whose lands and revenues
90   enrich the new duke. Therefore he gives them good leave to
wander.

OLIVER
Can you tell if Rosalind, the duke's daughter, be banished
with her father?

CHARLES
Oh, no, for the duke's daughter her cousin so loves her,
95   being ever from their cradles bred together, that she would
have followed her exile or have died to stay behind her. She
is at the court, and no less beloved of her uncle than his own
daughter, and never two ladies loved as they do.

OLIVER
Where will the old duke live?

CHARLES
100   They say he is already in the Forest of Arden, and a many
merry men with him; and there they live like the old Robin
Hood of England. They say many young gentlemen flock to
him every day and fleet the time carelessly, as they did in the
golden world.

OLIVER
105   What, you wrestle tomorrow before the new duke?

CHARLES

Good morning, sir.

OLIVER

Good Mr. Charles! Tell me, what's the latest news at the new court?

CHARLES

No news but the old news: the old Duke Senior has been banished by his younger brother, the new Duke Frederick. A few loyal lords have gone into exile with Duke Senior, and given up their lands and money to Frederick—so he's happy enough to have them leave.

OLIVER

Can you tell me whether Rosalind, Duke Senior's daughter, has also been banished?

CHARLES

Oh, no. Duke Frederick's daughter, Celia, grew up with Rosalind, and Celia loves her cousin so much that she would have either followed her into exile or died of grief. Rosalind has stayed at court, where Duke Frederick loves her like his own daughter. No two women ever loved each other like they do.

OLIVER

Where will the old duke live?

CHARLES

In Greek mythology, the first humans lived in a Golden Age, free from work, conflict, or violence, and without the need of laws.

They say he's already in the Forest of Arden. He has many cheerful men with him, and they live like Robin Hood and his outlaws. People say that new batches of young men flock there every day, and that they all pass the time without a care, like people did in the Golden Age.

OLIVER

So, are you going to wrestle before the new duke tomorrow?

CHARLES
Marry, do I, sir, and I came to acquaint you with a matter.
I am given, sir, secretly to understand that your younger
brother Orlando hath a disposition to come in disguised
against me to try a fall. Tomorrow, sir, I wrestle for my
110 credit, and he that escapes me without some broken limb
shall acquit him well. Your brother is but young and tender,
and, for your love I would be loath to foil him, as I must for
my own honor if he come in. Therefore, out of my love to
you, I came hither to acquaint you withal, that either you
115 might stay him from his intendment or brook such disgrace
well as he shall run into, in that it is a thing of his own search
and altogether against my will.

OLIVER
Charles, I thank thee for thy love to me, which thou shalt
find I will most kindly requite. I had myself notice of my
120 brother's purpose herein and have by underhand means
labored to dissuade him from it; but he is resolute. I'll tell
thee, Charles: it is the stubbornest young fellow of France,
full of ambition, an envious emulator of every man's good
parts, a secret and villainous contriver against me his
125 natural brother. Therefore use thy discretion. I had as lief
thou didst break his neck as his finger. And thou wert best
look to 't, for if thou dost him any slight disgrace or if he do
not mightily grace himself on thee, he will practice against
thee by poison, entrap thee by some treacherous device and
130 never leave thee till he hath ta'en thy life by some indirect
means or other. For I assure thee—and almost with tears I
speak it—there is not one so young and so villainous this
day living. I speak but brotherly of him, but should I
anatomize him to thee as he is, I must blush and weep, and
135 thou must look pale and wonder.

CHARLES

Indeed I do, sir, and I've come to let you in on a certain problem. I've been informed by certain sources I can't disclose that your younger brother Orlando plans to fight me in disguise. Tomorrow, sir, I'm fighting for my reputation, and any man who gets away without a broken bone or two is an exceptional wrestler indeed. Your brother is young and inexperienced, and because of my affection for you, I'd hate to crush him—though I'd have to, if he challenged me. I'm telling you all this out of affection for you, so you can either keep him from carrying out his plans or prepare to accept his disgrace, which will be his own fault, not mine.

OLIVER

Charles, I thank you for your loyalty to me, and you'll see that I'll reward you. I'd heard about my brother's plan and have been subtly trying to change his mind, but he's determined. I tell you, Charles, he's the stubbornest young fellow in France: overly ambitious, jealous of other people's good qualities, and a traitor against me, his own blood brother. So use your discretion. I'd be just as happy if you broke his neck as his finger. And you'd better be careful, because if you embarrass him at all—in fact, if he doesn't beat you thoroughly—he'll come after you and won't leave you alone till he's poisoned you or trapped you—killed you, in other words, one way or another. It brings me to tears to say this, but there isn't another person alive who is so young and at the same time so wicked. Because he's my brother, I have to take his side. But if I really laid him bare, I'd have to weep and hang my head, and you would not believe me, his behavior is so shocking.

CHARLES
I am heartily glad I came hither to you. If he come
tomorrow, I'll give him his payment. If ever he go alone
again, I'll never wrestle for prize more. And so God keep
your Worship.

OLIVER
140　　Farewell, good Charles.

Exit CHARLES

Now will I stir this gamester. I hope I shall see an end of
him, for my soul—yet I know not why—hates nothing
more than he. Yet he's gentle, never schooled and yet
learned, full of noble device, of all sorts enchantingly
145　　beloved, and indeed so much in the heart of the world and
especially of my own people, who best know him, that I am
altogether misprized. But it shall not be so long; this
wrestler shall clear all. Nothing remains but that I kindle
the boy thither, which now I'll go about.

Exit

CHARLES

> I'm very glad I came to see you. If he shows up tomorrow, I'll give him what's coming to him. If he can manage to walk after our fight, I'll never wrestle for money again. Farewell, my lord.

OLIVER

> Take care, Charles.

> *CHARLES exits.*

> Now it's time to get this playboy brother of mine all worked up. I hope I'll see the end of him soon—I don't know why, but I hate nothing in the world as much as him, though he's an upstanding guy. He's never gone to school but he's smart, with good values, and everyone is delighted by him and loves him, especially my subjects, who know him the best. They love him, and therefore they despise me. But not for long; Charles will take care of everything. All I have to do is get Orlando to fight, which I'll do now.

> *He exits.*

ACT 1, SCENE 2

Enter CELIA *and* ROSALIND

CELIA
I pray thee, Rosalind, sweet my coz, be merry.

ROSALIND
Dear Celia, I show more mirth than I am mistress of, and
would you yet I were merrier? Unless you could teach me to
forget a banished father, you must not learn me how to
5   remember any extraordinary pleasure.

CELIA
Herein I see thou lov'st me not with the full weight that I
love thee. If my uncle, thy banished father, had banished
thy uncle, the duke my father, so thou hadst been still with
me, I could have taught my love to take thy father for mine.
10   So wouldst thou, if the truth of thy love to me were so
righteously tempered as mine is to thee.

ROSALIND
Well, I will forget the condition of my estate to rejoice in
yours.

CELIA
You know my father hath no child but I, nor none is like to
15   have, and, truly, when he dies, thou shalt be his heir, for
what he hath taken away from thy father perforce, I will
render thee again in affection. By mine honor I will, and
when I break that oath, let me turn monster. Therefore, my
sweet Rose, my dear Rose, be merry.

ROSALIND
20   From henceforth I will, coz, and devise sports. Let me
see—what think you of falling in love?

CELIA
Marry, I prithee do, to make sport withal, but love no man
in good earnest, nor no further in sport neither than with
safety of a pure blush thou mayst in honor come off again.

ACT 1, SCENE 2

CELIA *and* ROSALIND *enter.*

CELIA

Please, Rosalind, my sweet cousin—be happy.

ROSALIND

Dear Celia—I already look much happier than I feel, but you want me to look even happier? Unless you can also teach me how to forget my banished father, you shouldn't try to teach me how to be happy.

CELIA

Well, by this I can see that you don't love me as much as I love you. If *your* father had banished my father, I could have learned to love your father as my own, as long as I still had you. You'd do the same, if your love for me were as true as mine for you.

ROSALIND

Well, I'll just forget the difficulties of my situation, in order to focus on the happiness of yours.

CELIA

You know I'm my father's only child, and he isn't likely to have another. And when he dies, you will inherit his fortune—because whatever he took from your father by force, I will return to you as affection. I swear I will, and if I ever break my promise let me turn into a monster. So please, my sweet Rose, my dear Rose, be happy.

ROSALIND

From now on I will, cousin, and I'll think of all kinds of games for us. Let me see—what do you think about falling in love?

CELIA

Yes, please do, so we can have a good laugh about it. But don't fall in love for real, and don't take the game too far. You want to get out of it easily, and with your honor intact.

ROSALIND

25   What shall be our sport, then?

CELIA

Let us sit and mock the good housewife Fortune from her
wheel, that her gifts may henceforth be bestowed equally.

ROSALIND

I would we could do so, for her benefits are mightily
misplaced, and the bountiful blind woman doth most

30   mistake in her gifts to women.

CELIA

'Tis true, for those that she makes fair she scarce makes
honest, and those that she makes honest she makes very ill-
favoredly.

ROSALIND

Nay, now thou goest from Fortune's office to Nature's.

35   Fortune reigns in gifts of the world, not in the lineaments of
Nature.

Enter TOUCHSTONE

CELIA

No? When Nature hath made a fair creature, may she not
by Fortune fall into the fire? Though Nature hath given us
wit to flout at Fortune, hath not Fortune sent in this fool to

40   cut off the argument?

ROSALIND

Indeed, there is Fortune too hard for Nature, when Fortune
makes Nature's natural the cutter-off of Nature's wit.

CELIA

Peradventure this is not Fortune's work neither, but
Nature's, who perceiveth our natural wits too dull to reason

45   of such goddesses, and hath sent this natural for our
whetstone, for always the dullness of the fool is the
whetstone of the wits. How now, wit, whither wander you?

ROSALIND

Well, then, what should we do for fun instead?

CELIA

Let's go find that hussy, Fortune, and and mock her till she starts distributing her gifts more equally.

ROSALIND

I wish we could do that, because Fortune gives all of her gifts to the wrong people, and she especially gets things wrong where women are concerned.

CELIA

It's true: the women she makes beautiful she also makes slutty, and the women she makes pure and virginal she also makes ugly.

ROSALIND

No, you're getting Fortune and Nature mixed up: Nature determines how we're made, and Fortune decides what happens to us.

TOUCHSTONE *enters.*

CELIA

Oh, really? Well, when Nature makes a person beautiful, can't Fortune make her fall into a fire, thereby making her ugly after all? And even though Nature has given us the wit to have this argument, hasn't Fortune sent this fool here to stop us?

ROSALIND

Yes, and now Fortune is playing a nasty trick on Nature: she's breaking up a show of wit between two naturally witty women with the arrival of a natural fool.

CELIA

Well, maybe this is Nature's work after all. Maybe Nature sensed that we're not smart enough to be having this high-flown discussion about goddesses, so she sent us this fool to use as a mental whetstone.

A whetstone is used to sharpen knives.

After all, smart peoples' wits are always sharpened by the presence of a fool. What's up, you wit? Where are you wandering off to?

TOUCHSTONE
    Mistress, you must come away to your father.

CELIA
    Were you made the messenger?

TOUCHSTONE
50   No, by mine honor, but I was bid to come for you.

ROSALIND
    Where learned you that oath, fool?

TOUCHSTONE
    Of a certain knight that swore by his honor they were good
    pancakes, and swore by his honor the mustard was naught.
    Now, I'll stand to it, the pancakes were naught and the
55   mustard was good, and yet was not the knight forsworn.

CELIA
    How prove you that in the great heap of your knowledge?

ROSALIND
    Ay, marry, now unmuzzle your wisdom.

TOUCHSTONE
    Stand you both forth now: stroke your chins and swear by
    your beards that I am a knave.

CELIA
60   By our beards (if we had them), thou art.

TOUCHSTONE
    By my knavery (if I had it), then I were. But if you swear by
    that that is not, you are not forsworn. No more was this
    knight swearing by his honor, for he never had any; or if he
    had, he had sworn it away before ever he saw those pancakes
65   or that mustard.

TOUCHSTONE

Mistress, you have to go see your father.

CELIA

Did they make you the messenger?

TOUCHSTONE

Touchstone is pretending that Celia meant, "Have you come to arrest us?" The term "messenger" was commonly used to describe someone who came with a warrant.

No, by my honor, but they told me to come get you.

ROSALIND

Where'd you learn a phrase like, "by my honor," fool?

TOUCHSTONE

From a certain knight who swore on his honor that the pancakes he was eating were good, and that the mustard on top of them—he swore on his honor—was bad. Now, I'll swear to the opposite—that the pancakes were rotten, and the mustard was fine—but even so, the knight wasn't lying.

CELIA

And how, out of your great heap of knowledge, will you manage to prove that?

ROSALIND

Yes, please; unleash your wisdom.

TOUCHSTONE

Watch me: stroke your chins and swear by your beards that I am a knave.

CELIA

By our beards (if we had them), you are a knave.

TOUCHSTONE

And I swear by my wickedness (if I had any) that I am a knave. But you can't swear by what you don't have—and this knight had no honor, or if he did, he swore it off before he ever saw those pancakes and that mustard.

CELIA
> Prithee, who is 't that thou mean'st?

TOUCHSTONE
> One that old Frederick, your father, loves.

CELIA
> My father's love is enough to honor him. Enough. Speak no
> more of him; you'll be whipped for taxation one of these
> days.

70

TOUCHSTONE
> The more pity that fools may not speak wisely what wise
> men do foolishly.

CELIA
> By my troth, thou sayest true. For, since the little wit that
> fools have was silenced, the little foolery that wise men have
> makes a great show. Here comes Monsieur Le Beau.

75

> *Enter* LE BEAU

ROSALIND
> With his mouth full of news.

CELIA
> Which he will put on us as pigeons feed their young.

ROSALIND
> Then shall we be news-crammed.

CELIA
> All the better. We shall be the more marketable.—Bonjour,
> Monsieur Le Beau. What's the news?

80

LE BEAU
> Fair princess, you have lost much good sport.

CELIA
> Sport? Of what color?

CELIA
Tell me, who is this knight?

TOUCHSTONE
A man old Frederick, your father, loves.

CELIA
If he has my father's love, then that's enough honor for me. Enough of this. No more talk about my father; you'll be whipped for slander one of these days.

TOUCHSTONE
It's a pity that fools aren't allowed to speak wisely about the foolish things that wise men do.

CELIA
Honestly, you're speaking the truth—ever since the fools were silenced, the foolishness of wise men has become all the more apparent. Here comes Monsieur Le Beau.

By "silencing" Celia may mean the burning of satirical books, in 1599.

LE BEAU enters.

ROSALIND
With his mouth full of news.

CELIA
Which he'll shove down our throats the way pigeons feed their young.

ROSALIND
Then we'll be stuffed with news.

CELIA
Well that's good. If we're fattened up, we'll be worth more.

A recently fed (and thus heavier) bird was worth more at the market.

Hello, Monsieur Le Beau. What's the news?

LE BEAU
Fair princess, you've missed some good sport.

CELIA
Sport? Of what color?

In other words, what kind of sport.

LE BEAU
What color, madam? How shall I answer you?

ROSALIND
As wit and fortune will.

TOUCHSTONE
85   Or as the Destinies decrees.

CELIA
Well said. That was laid on with a trowel.

TOUCHSTONE
Nay, if I keep not my rank—

ROSALIND
Thou losest thy old smell.

LE BEAU
You amaze me, ladies. I would have told you of good
90   wrestling, which you have lost the sight of.

ROSALIND
You tell us the manner of the wrestling.

LE BEAU
I will tell you the beginning, and if it please your
Ladyships, you may see the end, for the best is yet to do,
and here, where you are, they are coming to perform it.

CELIA
95   Well, the beginning that is dead and buried.

LE BEAU
There comes an old man and his three sons—

CELIA
I could match this beginning with an old tale.

LE BEAU
Three proper young men of excellent growth and presence.

LE BEAU

What color, madam? I don't understand—how should I answer that?

ROSALIND

However your wit and luck allow.

TOUCHSTONE

Or however the Destinies say you should.

CELIA

Nicely done; you laid *that* on thick.

TOUCHSTONE

Well, if I don't keep up my rank—

ROSALIND

—you'll lose your smell.

Touchstone means he has to keep up his reputation as a jester; Rosalind interprets "rank" as "foul smell."

LE BEAU

You're confusing me, ladies. I was going to tell you all about a good wrestling match that's going on, which you're missing.

ROSALIND

Tell us about this wrestling.

LE BEAU

I'll tell you about the beginning, and if you find that interesting you can see the end. The best is yet to come, and they're going to perform it right here.

CELIA

Well, we've missed the beginning; it's dead and buried.

LE BEAU

There comes an old man with his three sons—

CELIA

It sounds like the beginning of an old folktale.

LE BEAU

Three proper young men, all good looking and with great presence—

ROSALIND
With bills on their necks: "Be it known unto all men by
100   these presents."

LE BEAU
The eldest of the three wrestled with Charles, the duke's
wrestler, which Charles in a moment threw him and broke
three of his ribs, that there is little hope of life in him. So he
served the second, and so the third. Yonder they lie, the
105   poor old man their father making such pitiful dole over
them that all the beholders take his part with weeping.

ROSALIND
Alas!

TOUCHSTONE
But what is the sport, monsieur, that the ladies have lost?

LE BEAU
Why, this that I speak of.

TOUCHSTONE
110   Thus men may grow wiser every day. It is the first time that
ever I heard breaking of ribs was sport for ladies.

CELIA
Or I, I promise thee.

ROSALIND
But is there any else longs to see this broken music in his
sides? Is there yet another dotes upon rib-breaking? Shall
115   we see this wrestling, cousin?

ROSALIND

Right, and they wore proclamations around their necks, saying, "Be it known to all men by these presents—"

This is a phrase found at the beginning of legal documents. Rosalind is punning on the word "presence."

LE BEAU

The eldest of the three brothers wrestled with Charles, the duke's wrestler. Immediately, Charles threw the brother, breaking three of his ribs; it's not likely he will survive. Charles did the same to the second brother, and the third. They're lying over there, and the poor old man, their father, weeps so piteously over them that the whole audience has joined him in grieving.

ROSALIND

Oh, dear!

TOUCHSTONE

But tell me, monsieur—what sport are the ladies missing?

LE BEAU

Why, the one I just told you about.

TOUCHSTONE

Men must be getting wiser every day; that's the first time I've heard that rib-breaking was appropriate entertainment for ladies.

CELIA

Me too, I swear.

ROSALIND

Doesn't anyone else want to see this, and hear breath wheezing out from broken ribs? Does anyone else love rib breaking? Shall we go watch this wrestling, cousin?

LE BEAU
> You must if you stay here, for here is the place appointed for
> the wrestling, and they are ready to perform it.

CELIA
> Yonder sure they are coming. Let us now stay and see it.

Flourish. Enter DUKE FREDERICK, *lords,* ORLANDO,
CHARLES, *and attendants*

DUKE FREDERICK
> Come on. Since the youth will not be entreated, his own
> 120   peril on his forwardness.

ROSALIND
> Is yonder the man?

LE BEAU
> Even he, madam.

CELIA
> Alas, he is too young. Yet he looks successfully.

DUKE FREDERICK
> How now, daughter and cousin? Are you crept hither to see
> the wrestling?

ROSALIND
> Ay, my liege, so please you give us leave.

DUKE FREDERICK
> You will take little delight in it, I can tell you, there is such
> odds in the man. In pity of the challenger's youth, I would
> fain dissuade him, but he will not be entreated. Speak to
> him, ladies; see if you can move him.

CELIA
> Call him hither, good Monsieur Le Beau.

DUKE FREDERICK
> Do so. I'll not be by.

He steps aside.

LE BEAU

You're going to have to, if you stay here. This is the place they're scheduled to wrestle, and they're ready to go.

CELIA

Yes, I see them coming. Let's stay and watch.

Trumpets play. DUKE FREDERICK, *lords,* ORLANDO, CHARLES, *and attendants enter.*

DUKE FREDERICK

Come on. Since the youth won't be reasoned with, he'll have to suffer for his stubbornness.

ROSALIND

Is that the man?

LE BEAU

That's him, madam.

CELIA

Alas, he is too young. Yet he seems capable.

DUKE FREDERICK

What's up, daughter and niece? Have you snuck over here to watch the wrestling?

ROSALIND

Yes, my lord, if you give us permission.

DUKE FREDERICK

You won't enjoy it much, I can tell you, the odds are so against this young man. Because he's so young, I've tried to discourage him, but he won't listen. Talk to him, ladies. See if you can persuade him.

CELIA

Call him over here, good Monsieur Le Beau.

DUKE FREDERICK

Go ahead. I'll make myself scarce.

He steps aside.

LE BEAU
> Monsieur the challenger, the Princess calls for you.

ORLANDO
> I attend them with all respect and duty.

ROSALIND
135 > Young man, have you challenged Charles the wrestler?

ORLANDO
> No, fair princess. He is the general challenger. I come but
> in as others do, to try with him the strength of my youth.

CELIA
> Young gentleman, your spirits are too bold for your years.
> You have seen cruel proof of this man's strength. If you saw
140 > yourself with your eyes or knew yourself with your
> judgment, the fear of your adventure would counsel you to
> a more equal enterprise. We pray you for your own sake to
> embrace your own safety and give over this attempt.

ROSALIND
> Do, young sir. Your reputation shall not therefore be
145 > misprized. We will make it our suit to the duke that the
> wrestling might not go forward.

ORLANDO
> I beseech you, punish me not with your hard thoughts,
> wherein I confess me much guilty to deny so fair and
> excellent ladies anything. But let your fair eyes and gentle
150 > wishes go with me to my trial, wherein, if I be foiled, there
> is but one shamed that was never gracious; if killed, but one
> dead that was willing to be so. I shall do my friends no
> wrong, for I have none to lament me; the world no injury,
> for in it I have nothing. Only in the world I fill up a place
155 > which may be better supplied when I have made it empty.

ROSALIND
> The little strength that I have, I would it were with you.

CELIA
> And mine, to eke out hers.

LE BEAU

Mister Challenger, the princess wants to speak to you.

ORLANDO

I'll wait on them with all respect and duty.

ROSALIND

Young man, have you challenged Charles the Wrestler?

ORLANDO

No, lovely princess. He is the general challenger. I have only come in—like the others have—to try to fight him with the strength of my youth.

CELIA

Young gentleman, you are too bold for your age. You have seen the cruel proof of this man's strength. If you took a good look at yourself, or if you thought about this more carefully, your fear would teach you to act more cautiously. We beg you, for your own sake, to respect your safety and give up.

ROSALIND

Please, young sir. We'll make sure your reputation isn't hurt; we'll take it upon ourselves to argue with the duke that the wrestling match should be called off.

ORLANDO

I beg you not to think poorly of me—though I suppose anyone who could deny anything to such beautiful women deserves to be scorned. But please, send me good thoughts in this match. If I'm beaten, the shame is all mine, and I wasn't in anyone's good graces to begin with. If I'm killed, it will only be the death of a man who was willing to be dead. I won't wrong any of my friends, because I don't have any to mourn for me, and I won't have wronged the world, because I don't have anything in the world. In this world, I'm only taking up space. If I leave, maybe someone more worthy will fill it.

ROSALIND

I wish I could give you the little strength that I have.

CELIA

Mine too, to join hers.

ROSALIND
>Fare you well. Pray heaven I be deceived in you.

CELIA
>Your heart's desires be with you.

CHARLES
160 >Come, where is this young gallant that is so desirous to lie
>with his mother earth?

ORLANDO
>Ready, sir; but his will hath in it a more modest working.

DUKE FREDERICK
>You shall try but one fall.

CHARLES
>No, I warrant your Grace you shall not entreat him to a
165 >second, that have so mightily persuaded him from a first.

ORLANDO
>You mean to mock me after, you should not have mocked
>me before. But come your ways.

ROSALIND
>Now Hercules be thy speed, young man!

CELIA
>I would I were invisible, to catch the strong fellow by the
170 >leg.

>*They wrestle*

ROSALIND
>O excellent young man!

ROSALIND

Good luck. I hope to God I'm wrong about your chances.

CELIA

I hope you get what you desire!

CHARLES

Charles is asking "Who wants to be buried?" as well as making a suggestive pun.

Come on, where's the young show-off who's so eager to lie with mother earth?

ORLANDO

Ready, sir, but I have more modest ambitions.

DUKE FREDERICK

You get only one round.

CHARLES

No, I'm sure your Grace won't be able to persuade him to try a second round, even though you couldn't dissuade him from trying the first.

ORLANDO

You should mock me *after* you've beaten me, not before. Come on.

ROSALIND

Hercules, a prominent figure in Greek and Roman mythology, was famous for his physical prowess.

Hercules give you speed, young man!

CELIA

I wish I were invisible, so I could grab that strong fellow by the leg.

They wrestle.

ROSALIND

Oh, what an excellent young man!

CELIA

> If I had a thunderbolt in mine eye, I can tell who should
> down.

CHARLES is thrown
Shout

DUKE FREDERICK

> No more, no more.

ORLANDO

175 Yes, I beseech your Grace. I am not yet well breathed.

DUKE FREDERICK

> How dost thou, Charles?

LE BEAU

> He cannot speak, my lord.

DUKE FREDERICK

> Bear him away. What is thy name, young man?

ORLANDO

> Orlando, my liege, the youngest son of Sir Rowland de
180 Boys.

DUKE FREDERICK

> I would thou hadst been son to some man else.
> The world esteemed thy father honorable,
> But I did find him still mine enemy.
> Thou shouldst have better pleased me with this deed
185 Hadst thou descended from another house.
> But fare thee well. Thou art a gallant youth.
> I would thou hadst told me of another father.

Exeunt DUKE FREDERICK, train, and LE BEAU

CELIA

> Were I my father, coz, would I do this?

ORLANDO

> I am more proud to be Sir Rowland's son,
190 His youngest son, and would not change that calling
> To be adopted heir to Frederick.

CELIA

> If I could shoot lightning bolts from my eyes, I can tell you who'd be on the ground.

ORLANDO *throws Charles. The crowd shouts.*

DUKE FREDERICK

> No more, no more.

ORLANDO

> Oh, come on, your Grace—I'm barely out of breath.

DUKE FREDERICK

> How are you doing, Charles?

LE BEAU

> He can't speak, my lord.

DUKE FREDERICK

> Carry him away. What is your name, young man?

ORLANDO

> Orlando, my lord, the youngest son of Sir Rowland de Boys.

DUKE FREDERICK

> I wish you were someone else's son. The whole world thought your father was an honorable man, but he was always my enemy. Your victory would have pleased me more if you'd been someone else's son. But good luck; you are a brave young man. I wish you had told me you had a different father.

DUKE FREDERICK, *his train, and* LE BEAU *exit.*

CELIA

> If I were my father, cousin, would I do this?

ORLANDO

> I'm proud to be Sir Rowland's son—his youngest son—and I would never change that, not even to be Frederick's adopted heir.

ROSALIND

My father loved Sir Rowland as his soul,
And all the world was of my father's mind.
Had I before known this young man his son,
195   I should have given him tears unto entreaties
Ere he should thus have ventured.

CELIA

Gentle cousin,
Let us go thank him and encourage him.
My father's rough and envious disposition
200   Sticks me at heart.—Sir, you have well deserved.
If you do keep your promises in love
But justly, as you have exceeded all promise,
Your mistress shall be happy.

ROSALIND

Gentleman, *(giving him a chain from her neck)*
205   Wear this for me—one out of suits with fortune
That could give more but that her hand lacks means.
—Shall we go, coz?

CELIA

Ay.—Fare you well, fair gentleman.

ORLANDO

Can I not say "I thank you"? My better parts
210   Are all thrown down, and that which here stands up
Is but a quintain, a mere lifeless block.

ROSALIND

He calls us back. My pride fell with my fortunes.
I'll ask him what he would.—Did you call, sir?
Sir, you have wrestled well and overthrown
215   More than your enemies.

CELIA

Will you go, coz?

ROSALIND

Have with you. Fare you well.

Exeunt **ROSALIND** *and* **CELIA**

ROSALIND

My father loved Sir Rowland as much as he loved his own soul, and the rest of the world shared my father's opinion. If I had known this young man was his son, I would have tried harder to convince him not to fight.

CELIA

Gentle cousin, let's go thank him and encourage him. My my father's rude and envious behavior is like a knife through my heart. *(to ORLANDO)* Sir, you fought very well. If you live up to your potential in love as well, your wife will be a very happy woman.

ROSALIND

(giving him a chain from her neck) Gentleman, wear this for me. I'm a woman who's down on her luck, and I'd give more if I could. Shall we go, cousin?

CELIA

Yes. Good luck, fair gentleman.

ORLANDO

(to himself) Can't I even say "thank you"? I left my brain back on the wrestling field. What's left of me is a dummy, just a lifeless block.

ROSALIND

Rosalind implies that he conquered her as well, in the sense that she's fallen in love with him.

He's calling us back. My pride fell when my fortunes did; I'll ask him what he wants.—Did you call us, sir? Sir, you wrestled well and conquered more than just your enemies.

CELIA

Will you come on, cousin?

ROSALIND

I'm coming. Farewell.

ROSALIND *and* CELIA *exit.*

ORLANDO

What passion hangs these weights upon my tongue?
I cannot speak to her, yet she urged conference.
220   O poor Orlando! Thou art overthrown.
Or Charles or something weaker masters thee.

Enter LE BEAU

LE BEAU

Good sir, I do in friendship counsel you
To leave this place. Albeit you have deserved
High commendation, true applause, and love,
225   Yet such is now the duke's condition
That he misconsters all that you have done.
The duke is humorous. What he is indeed
More suits you to conceive than I to speak of.

ORLANDO

I thank you, sir, and pray you tell me this:
230   Which of the two was daughter of the duke
That here was at the wrestling?

LE BEAU

Neither his daughter, if we judge by manners,
But yet indeed the smaller is his daughter
The other is daughter to the banished duke,
235   And here detained by her usurping uncle
To keep his daughter company, whose loves
Are dearer than the natural bond of sisters.
But I can tell you that of late this duke
Hath ta'en displeasure 'gainst his gentle niece,
240   Grounded upon no other argument
But that the people praise her for her virtues
And pity her for her good father's sake;
And, on my life, his malice 'gainst the lady
Will suddenly break forth. Sir, fare you well.
245   Hereafter, in a better world than this,
I shall desire more love and knowledge of you.

ORLANDO

What is this passion that ties up my tongue? I can't speak to her, even though she asked me to. Oh, poor Orlando, you've been overthrown! Either Charles or some prettier thing has mastered you.

LE BEAU *enters.*

LE BEAU

Good sir, as a friend, I advise you to leave this place. Although you deserve praise, applause, and love, right now the duke misconstrues everything you've done. The duke is temperamental. I'm sure you can imagine what I mean without my having to spell it out.

ORLANDO

Thank you, sir. Now please tell me this: which of the two ladies who were at the wrestling match is the duke's daughter?

LE BEAU

Neither one is his daughter, to judge from their good manners. But really, the smaller one is his daughter. The other is the daughter of the banished duke. Duke Frederick keeps her for his daughter's sake; the love between the two of them is stronger than the bond between sisters. But I will tell you that lately the duke has been displeased with his niece, and for no other reason than that people praise her virtues and pity her for her father's sake. I swear, one day the duke's malice toward Rosalind will suddenly erupt. Goodbye, sir. Later, in a better world than this, I'd love to get to know you.

ORLANDO
I rest much bounden to you. Fare you well.

Exit LE BEAU

Thus must I from the smoke into the smother,
From tyrant duke unto a tyrant brother.
250   But heavenly Rosalind!

Exit

ORLANDO

I'm indebted to you. Goodbye.

LE BEAU exits.

Out of the frying pan and into the fire—from a tyrant duke to a tyrant brother! But, oh, heavenly Rosalind!

He exits.

ACT 1, SCENE 3

Enter CELIA *and* ROSALIND

CELIA

Why, cousin! Why, Rosalind! Cupid have mercy, not a
word?

ROSALIND

Not one to throw at a dog.

CELIA

No, thy words are too precious to be cast away upon curs.
Throw some of them at me. Come, lame me with reasons.

ROSALIND

Then there were two cousins laid up, when the one should
be lamed with reasons and the other mad without any.

CELIA

But is all this for your father?

ROSALIND

No, some of it is for my child's father. Oh, how full of briers
is this working-day world!

CELIA

They are but burs, cousin, thrown upon thee in holiday
foolery. If we walk not in the trodden paths our very
petticoats will catch them.

ROSALIND

I could shake them off my coat. These burs are in my heart.

CELIA

Hem them away.

ROSALIND

I would try, if I could cry "hem" and have him.

CELIA

Come, come, wrestle with thy affections.

ACT 1, SCENE 3

CELIA *and* ROSALIND *enter.*

CELIA

What's going on, Rosalind? Cupid have mercy! You won't utter a single word?

ROSALIND

I don't even have one to throw at a dog.

CELIA

No, your words are too precious to be wasted on dogs. Throw some of your words at me. Come on, throw your words at me like you would throw stones at a dog.

ROSALIND

Then there would be two cousins lying sick in bed: one hurt by reasons and the other gone crazy without any.

CELIA

Is all of this about your father?

ROSALIND

No, some of it is about my child's father. Oh, this working-day world is full of thorns!

Working-day= wearisome.

CELIA

They're only burrs, cousin, thrown at you because you took a holiday from conventional behavior. If we walk on the well-worn paths, they won't get caught in our petticoats.

ROSALIND

Those burrs I could shake off my clothing, but these are in my heart.

CELIA

Cough them up.

ROSALIND

I'd try it, if I could cry "hem" and have him.

CELIA

Come on, take control of your feelings.

ROSALIND
> Oh, they take the part of a better wrestler than myself.

CELIA
> Oh, a good wish upon you. You will try in time, in despite
> of a fall. But turning these jests out of service, let us talk in
> good earnest. Is it possible on such a sudden you should fall
> into so strong a liking with old Sir Rowland's youngest son?

ROSALIND
> The duke my father loved his father dearly.

CELIA
> Doth it therefore ensue that you should love his son dearly?
> By this kind of chase I should hate him, for my father hated
> his father dearly. Yet I hate not Orlando.

ROSALIND
> No, faith, hate him not, for my sake.

CELIA
> Why should I not? Doth he not deserve well?

ROSALIND
> Let me love him for that, and do you love him because I do.
> Look, here comes the duke.

Enter DUKE FREDERICK *with lords*

CELIA
> With his eyes full of anger.

DUKE FREDERICK
> Mistress, dispatch you with your safest haste,
> And get you from our court.

ROSALIND
> Me, uncle?

DUKE FREDERICK
> You, cousin.
> Within these ten days if that thou beest found
> So near our public court as twenty miles,
> Thou diest for it.

ROSALIND

But they're siding with a better wrestler than myself.

CELIA

Oh, that's a good wish! You'll fight with him eventually, and fall. But let's put these jokes aside for a moment, and speak earnestly. Is it possible that you could have fallen in love with Orlando, Sir Rowland's youngest son, this suddenly?

Celia means both that Rosalind will be "defeated" by her affections for Orlando and that she will "fall" to him sexually.

ROSALIND

The duke, my father, loved his father very much.

CELIA

Does that necessarily mean you should love his son? By that kind of logic, I should hate Orlando, since my father hates his father. But I don't hate Orlando.

ROSALIND

No, please don't hate him—for my sake.

CELIA

Why shouldn't I? Doesn't he deserve it?

ROSALIND

Let me love him because he deserves it, and you can love him because I do. Look, here comes the duke.

DUKE FREDERICK *enters, with lords*

CELIA

He looks angry.

DUKE FREDERICK

Madam, hurry as fast as you can get out of my court.

ROSALIND

Me, uncle?

DUKE FREDERICK

You, niece. In ten days time, if you're found within twenty miles of the court, you'll die for it.

ROSALIND
> I do beseech your Grace,
> Let me the knowledge of my fault bear with me.
> If with myself I hold intelligence
> Or have acquaintance with mine own desires,
> If that I do not dream or be not frantic—
> As I do trust I am not—then, dear uncle,
> Never so much as in a thought unborn
> Did I offend your Highness.

DUKE FREDERICK
> Thus do all traitors.
> If their purgation did consist in words,
> They are as innocent as grace itself.
> Let it suffice thee that I trust thee not.

ROSALIND
> Yet your mistrust cannot make me a traitor.
> Tell me whereon the likelihood depends.

DUKE FREDERICK
> Thou art thy father's daughter. There's enough.

ROSALIND
> So was I when your Highness took his dukedom.
> So was I when your Highness banished him.
> Treason is not inherited, my lord,
> Or if we did derive it from our friends,
> What's that to me? My father was no traitor.
> Then, good my liege, mistake me not so much
> To think my poverty is treacherous.

CELIA
> Dear sovereign, hear me speak.

DUKE FREDERICK
> Ay, Celia, we stayed her for your sake.
> Else had she with her father ranged along.

ROSALIND

Please, your Grace, tell me what crime I have committed. If I know my own thoughts and desires, and I'm not dreaming or crazy—which I'm sure I'm not—then, dear uncle, I've never had so much as a half-formed thought that would have offended you.

DUKE FREDERICK

All traitors protest like this. If they could purge their guilt simply by saying that they were innocent, they'd all be as innocent as God Himself. I don't trust you. Enough said.

ROSALIND

But your mistrust alone can't make me a traitor—on what basis do you suspect me?

DUKE FREDERICK

You are your father's daughter. That's enough.

ROSALIND

I was his daughter when your Highness took my father's dukedom. I was his daughter when you banished him. Treason is not inherited, my lord. But even if we did inherit it from our family, what does that have to do with me? My father wasn't a traitor. So, please, my lord, don't assume that I'm treacherous just because I'm poor, with no titles to my name.

CELIA

Dear master, listen to me.

DUKE FREDERICK

Yes, Celia, we kept her here for your sake. Otherwise, she would have been banished with her father.

CELIA

I did not then entreat to have her stay.

65 It was your pleasure and your own remorse.

I was too young that time to value her,

But now I know her. If she be a traitor,

Why so am I. We still have slept together,

Rose at an instant, learned, played, eat together,

70 And, wheresoe'er we went, like Juno's swans

Still we went coupled and inseparable.

DUKE FREDERICK

She is too subtle for thee, and her smoothness,

Her very silence and her patience

Speak to the people, and they pity her.

75 Thou art a fool. She robs thee of thy name,

And thou wilt show more bright and seem more virtuous

When she is gone. Then open not thy lips.

Firm and irrevocable is my doom

Which I have passed upon her. She is banished.

CELIA

80 Pronounce that sentence then on me, my liege.

I cannot live out of her company.

DUKE FREDERICK

You are a fool.—You, niece, provide yourself.

If you outstay the time, upon mine honor

And in the greatness of my word, you die.

Exeunt DUKE FREDERICK *and lords*

CELIA

85 O my poor Rosalind, whither wilt thou go?

Wilt thou change fathers? I will give thee mine.

I charge thee, be not thou more grieved than I am.

ROSALIND

I have more cause.

CELIA

At that time, I didn't beg you to keep her here; you wanted her here, and you felt guilty. I was too young at the time to appreciate her value, but now I know her. If she's a traitor, why then, so am I. We have always slept together, woken up together, learned, played, and eaten together. Wherever we went, we went together and inseparable.

DUKE FREDERICK

She's too devious for you. Her smoothness, her silence, and her patient suffering appeal to the people, and they pity her. You're a fool. She's robbing you of the attention you deserve. You will seem even brighter and more virtuous when she's out of the picture. So be quiet. The sentence I've passed down on her is firm and unshakeable. She is banished.

CELIA

Then lay that sentence on me too, my lord. I cannot live without her.

DUKE FREDERICK

You are a fool.—You, niece, prepare to leave. On my honor and by my word, if you outstay the ten days, you will die.

DUKE FREDERICK *and lords exit.*

CELIA

Oh, my poor Rosalind, where will you go? Do you want to exchange fathers? I'll give you mine. I insist, don't be more distressed than I am.

ROSALIND

I have more reason to be distressed.

CELIA
Thou hast not, cousin.
90   Prithee, be cheerful. Know'st thou not the duke
Hath banished me, his daughter?

ROSALIND
That he hath not.

CELIA
No, hath not? Rosalind lacks then the love
Which teacheth thee that thou and I am one.
95   Shall we be sundered? Shall we part, sweet girl?
No, let my father seek another heir.
Therefore devise with me how we may fly,
Whither to go, and what to bear with us,
And do not seek to take your change upon you,
100   To bear your griefs yourself and leave me out.
For, by this heaven, now at our sorrows pale,
Say what thou canst, I'll go along with thee.

ROSALIND
Why, whither shall we go?

CELIA
To seek my uncle in the Forest of Arden.

ROSALIND
105   Alas, what danger will it be to us,
Maids as we are, to travel forth so far?
Beauty provoketh thieves sooner than gold.

CELIA
I'll put myself in poor and mean attire
And with a kind of umber smirch my face.
110   The like do you. So shall we pass along
And never stir assailants.

ROSALIND
Were it not better,
Because that I am more than common tall,
That I did suit me all points like a man?

CELIA

No you haven't, cousin. Please, be cheerful. Don't you realize the duke has also banished me, his daughter?

ROSALIND

No, he hasn't.

CELIA

Oh, he hasn't? Well, then, you don't have the affection that would teach you that you and I are one. Will we be separated? Should we part, sweet girl? No. Let my father find another heir. So, help me plan how we'll escape, where we'll go, and what we'll take with us. Don't even try to take this all upon yourself, bearing your grief alone and leaving me out. I swear by the heavens, which have grown pale in sympathy with us, I'm going with you, whatever you say.

ROSALIND

But where will we go?

CELIA

To the Forest of Arden, to find your father.

ROSALIND

But what danger we'll put ourselves in, two young, innocent women traveling so far! Fresh beauty attracts thugs and thieves even more than money.

CELIA

I'll put on some poor and ragged clothes and smudge my face with dirt. You do the same, and we'll be able to travel without attracting any attackers' attention.

ROSALIND

Wouldn't it be better—since I'm unusually tall for a woman—to dress myself like a man?

115 A gallant curtal-axe upon my thigh,
A boar-spear in my hand, and in my heart
Lie there what hidden woman's fear there will,
We'll have a swashing and a martial outside—
As many other mannish cowards have
120 That do outface it with their semblances.

CELIA
What shall I call thee when thou art a man?

ROSALIND
I'll have no worse a name than Jove's own page,
And therefore look you call me Ganymede.
But what will you be called?

CELIA
125 Something that hath a reference to my state:
No longer Celia, but Aliena.

ROSALIND
But, cousin, what if we assayed to steal
The clownish fool out of your father's court?
Would he not be a comfort to our travel?

CELIA
130 He'll go along o'er the wide world with me.
Leave me alone to woo him. Let's away
And get our jewels and our wealth together,
Devise the fittest time and safest way
To hide us from pursuit that will be made
135 After my flight. Now go we in content
To liberty, and not to banishment.

Exeunt

I'll wear a big sword in my belt, carry a boar-spear in my hand, and hide all my womanish fear in my heart. We'll maintain a swaggering, warrior look, like so many cowardly men, whose manner has nothing to do with what they're feeling.

CELIA

What should I call you when you're a man?

ROSALIND

In Classical mythology, Jove, king of the gods, fell in love with the mortal boy Ganymede and carried him to Mt. Olympus to be his cup bearer.

I'll take no lesser name than that of Jove's own servant. So call me Ganymede. And what will you be called?

CELIA

Something that refers to my current state. Instead of Celia, call me Aliena.

ROSALIND

Cousin, what if we brought that clownish fool of your father's court, Touchstone? Wouldn't he be a comfort to us in our travels?

CELIA

He'd walk the whole wide world with me. Leave me alone to go convince him. Let's go gather our jewels and money. We'll figure out the best time and safest route to avoid being found out by my father's guards, whom he'll send out as soon as he discovers I've gone. Now, we go contentedly to freedom—not banishment.

They exit.

ACT TWO

SCENE 1

Enter DUKE SENIOR, AMIENS, *and two or three* LORDS, *like foresters*

DUKE SENIOR
Now, my co-mates and brothers in exile,
Hath not old custom made this life more sweet
Than that of painted pomp? Are not these woods
More free from peril than the envious court?
5   Here feel we not the penalty of Adam,
The seasons' difference, as the icy fang
And churlish chiding of the winter's wind,
Which, when it bites and blows upon my body,
Even till I shrink with cold, I smile and say,
10   "This is no flattery. These are counselors
That feelingly persuade me what I am."
Sweet are the uses of adversity,
Which, like the toad, ugly and venomous,
Wears yet a precious jewel in his head.
15   And this our life, exempt from public haunt,
Finds tongues in trees, books in the running brooks,
Sermons in stones, and good in everything.

AMIENS
I would not change it. Happy is your Grace,
That can translate the stubbornness of fortune
20   Into so quiet and so sweet a style.

DUKE SENIOR
Come, shall we go and kill us venison?
And yet it irks me the poor dappled fools,
Being native burghers of this desert city,
Should in their own confines with forkèd heads
25   Have their round haunches gored.

ACT TWO
SCENE 1

DUKE SENIOR, AMIENS, *and two or three* LORDS *enter, dressed like foresters.*

DUKE SENIOR

Now, my companions and brothers in exile, hasn't experience made this simple life sweeter than a life of glittery pomp and circumstance? Aren't these woods less perilous than the court, with all its jealousies and intrigues? Out here we feel the changing of the seasons, but we're not bothered by it. When the icy fangs of the brutal, scolding wind bite and blow on my body, even though I'm shivering with cold, I can appreciate the weather's honesty. I smile and think, "Thank goodness the wind doesn't flatter me: it's like a councilor who makes me feel what I'm really made of." Adversity can have its benefits—like the ugly, poisonous toad that wears a precious jewel in its forehead. In this life, far away from the civilized world, we can hear the language of the trees, read the books of the running streams, hear sermons in the stones, and discover the good in every single thing.

Toads were thought to be poisonous, and to each have a jewel embedded in its forehead.

AMIENS

I wouldn't change my situation for anything. You're lucky, my lord, to be able to see the peace and sweetness even in what bad luck has brought you.

DUKE SENIOR

Come, shall we hunt some deer for dinner? It bothers me, though, that these poor spotted innocents, who, after all, are this deserted city's native citizens, should be gouged with arrows.

FIRST LORD
Indeed, my lord,
The melancholy Jaques grieves at that,
And in that kind swears you do more usurp
Than doth your brother that hath banished you.
30   Today my Lord of Amiens and myself
Did steal behind him as he lay along
Under an oak, whose antique root peeps out
Upon the brook that brawls along this wood,
To the which place a poor sequestered stag
35   That from the hunter's aim had ta'en a hurt
Did come to languish. And indeed, my lord,
The wretched animal heaved forth such groans
That their discharge did stretch his leathern coat
Almost to bursting, and the big round tears
40   Coursed one another down his innocent nose
In piteous chase. And thus the hairy fool,
Much markèd of the melancholy Jaques,
Stood on th' extremest verge of the swift brook,
Augmenting it with tears.

DUKE SENIOR
45   But what said Jaques?
Did he not moralize this spectacle?

FIRST LORD
Oh, yes, into a thousand similes.
First, for his weeping into the needless stream:
"Poor deer," quoth he, "thou mak'st a testament
50   As worldlings do, giving thy sum of more
To that which had too much." Then, being there alone,
Left and abandoned of his velvet friend,
"'Tis right," quoth he. "Thus misery doth part
The flux of company." Anon a careless herd,
55   Full of the pasture, jumps along by him
And never stays to greet him. "Ay," quoth Jaques,
"Sweep on, you fat and greasy citizens.

FIRST LORD

Indeed, my lord, the gloomy Jaques grieves over these deaths. He swears that when you kill the deer, you're a worse usurper than your brother was for banishing you. Today, Lord Amiens and I followed Jaques. We saw him lie down along a brook under an oak tree whose ancient roots peeked out from the earth. A poor, lonely stag who had been hurt by a hunter's arrow came to rest there, where he heaved such heavy groans that the effort seemed to stretch his hide to bursting. Big, round tears ran piteously down the animal's innocent nose. The hairy fool, watched closely by sad Jaques, stood on the very edge of the brook, adding his own tears to the streaming water.

DUKE SENIOR

And what did Jaques say? Didn't he take the opportunity to draw a moral from the scene?

FIRST LORD

Oh, yes, he created a thousand comparisons. First, he spoke of the deer's needless addition to the stream's water supply. "Poor deer," he said, "you're just like a human: you add more to what already has too much." Then, about the deer's being alone, abandoned by his velvety companions: "It's appropriate," he said, "that a miserable creature should excuse itself from company." Just then, a carefree herd of deer, having just eaten their fill of pasture grass, bounded along without stopping to greet their wounded brother. "Sure," said Jaques, "hurry on, you fat and greasy citizens.

'Tis just the fashion. Wherefore do you look
Upon that poor and broken bankrupt there?"
60   Thus most invectively he pierceth through
The body of the country, city, court,
Yea, and of this our life, swearing that we
Are mere usurpers, tyrants, and what's worse,
To fright the animals and to kill them up
65   In their assigned and native dwelling place.

DUKE SENIOR
And did you leave him in this contemplation?

SECOND LORD
We did, my lord, weeping and commenting
Upon the sobbing deer.

DUKE SENIOR
Show me the place.
70   I love to cope him in these sullen fits,
For then he's full of matter.

FIRST LORD
I'll bring you to him straight.

Exeunt

Why stop and notice this poor, broken, bankrupt creature here?" In this way, he most insightfully pierced to the heart of the country, the city, the court, and even our lives out here in the forest, swearing that we are mere usurpers and tyrants, frightening and killing animals in their own homes.

DUKE SENIOR

And did you leave him like this?

SECOND LORD

We did, my lord, weeping and carrying on about the sobbing deer.

DUKE SENIOR

Take me to him. I love to argue with him when he's having one of these fits, because then he always has a lot to say.

FIRST LORD

I'll bring you to him right away.

They all exit.

ACT 2, SCENE 2

Enter DUKE FREDERICK, *with* LORDS

DUKE FREDERICK
      Can it be possible that no man saw them?
      It cannot be. Some villains of my court
      Are of consent and sufferance in this.

FIRST LORD
      I cannot hear of any that did see her.
5   The ladies, her attendants of her chamber
      Saw her abed, and in the morning early
      They found the bed untreasured of their mistress.

SECOND LORD
      My lord, the roinish clown, at whom so oft
      Your Grace was wont to laugh, is also missing.
10   Hisperia, the Princess' gentlewoman,
      Confesses that she secretly o'erheard
      Your daughter and her cousin much commend
      The parts and graces of the wrestler
      That did but lately foil the sinewy Charles,
15   And she believes wherever they are gone
      That youth is surely in their company.

DUKE FREDERICK
      Send to his brother. Fetch that gallant hither.
      If he be absent, bring his brother to me.
      I'll make him find him. Do this suddenly,
20   And let not search and inquisition quail
      To bring again these foolish runaways.

Exeunt

ACT 2, SCENE 2

DUKE FREDERICK *enters, with* LORDS

DUKE FREDERICK
>Can it be possible that no one saw them leave? It cannot be. Some villains in my court must have known about this and let it happen.

FIRST LORD
>I can't find anyone who saw her leave. Her ladies-in-waiting saw her go to bed, and early this morning the bed was empty.

SECOND LORD
>My lord, that dirty clown whom you laughed at so often is also missing. Hisperia, the princess's gentlewoman, confesses that she overheard your daughter and her cousin praising the good looks and skills of the wrestler who recently beat the muscular Charles. Hisperia believes that, wherever they have gone, that young man is likely with them.

DUKE FREDERICK
>Send a message to his brother. Bring that swinger Orlando here. If he's not around, bring his brother Oliver to me. I'll make Oliver find him. Do this immediately, and don't stop searching and interrogating until you've brought home these foolish runaways.

>*They all exit.*

ACT 2, SCENE 3

Enter ORLANDO *and* ADAM, *meeting*

ORLANDO
Who's there?

ADAM
What, my young master, O my gentle master,
O my sweet master, O you memory
Of old Sir Rowland! Why, what make you here?
5   Why are you virtuous? Why do people love you?
And wherefore are you gentle, strong, and valiant?
Why would you be so fond to overcome
The bonny prizer of the humorous duke?
Your praise is come too swiftly home before you.
10   Know you not, master, to some kind of men
Their graces serve them but as enemies?
No more do yours. Your virtues, gentle master,
Are sanctified and holy traitors to you.
Oh, what a world is this when what is comely
15   Envenoms him that bears it!

ORLANDO
Why, what's the matter?

ADAM
O unhappy youth,
Come not within these doors. Within this roof
The enemy of all your graces lives.
20   Your brother—no, no brother—yet the son—
Yet not the son, I will not call him son—
Of him I was about to call his father
Hath heard your praises, and this night he means
To burn the lodging where you use to lie,
25   And you within it. If he fail of that,
He will have other means to cut you off.
I overheard him and his practices.
This is no place, this house is but a butchery.
Abhor it, fear it, do not enter it.

ACT 2, SCENE 3

ORLANDO *and* ADAM *enter from opposite sides of the stage.*

ORLANDO

Who's there?

ADAM

My young master! Oh, my gentle master! My sweet master! Oh, you living memory of old Sir Rowland! What are you doing here? Why are you so strong and good? Why do people love you? And why are you noble, strong, and brave? Why would you be so foolish as to beat the moody duke's favorite champion? Your praise has beaten you home. Don't you know, master, that some men's best qualities do them in? Yours are like that—complete and utter traitors to you. Oh, what a world this is, when even what is beautiful in a man poisons him!

ORLANDO

Why, what's the matter?

ADAM

Oh, unlucky boy! Don't walk through these doors. In this house lives a man who despises all that is good in you. Oliver, your brother—no, not your brother; and yet he's the son—but no, I won't call him the son—of that great man I was about to call his father, has heard about how well you did in the wrestling match, and tonight he's planning on burning your house down, with you in it. And if he fails at that, he will find other ways to kill you. I overheard him and his plans. This is no place for you; this home is now a slaughterhouse. Hate it, fear it, do not come inside.

ORLANDO
30 Why, whither, Adam, wouldst thou have me go?

ADAM
No matter whither, so you come not here.

ORLANDO
What, wouldst thou have me go and beg my food,
Or with a base and boist'rous sword enforce
A thievish living on the common road?
35 This I must do, or know not what to do.
Yet this I will not do, do how I can.
I rather will subject me to the malice
Of a diverted blood and bloody brother.

ADAM
But do not so. I have five hundred crowns,
40 The thrifty hire I saved under your father,
Which I did store to be my foster nurse
When service should in my old limbs lie lame
And unregarded age in corners thrown.
Take that, and He that doth the ravens feed,
45 Yea, providently caters for the sparrow,
Be comfort to my age. Here is the gold.
All this I give you. Let me be your servant.
Though I look old, yet I am strong and lusty,
For in my youth I never did apply
50 Hot and rebellious liquors in my blood
Nor did not with unbashful forehead woo
The means of weakness and debility.
Therefore my age is as a lusty winter,
Frosty but kindly. Let me go with you.
55 I'll do the service of a younger man
In all your business and necessities.

ORLANDO

Then where would you have me go, Adam?

ADAM

It doesn't matter where, so long as it's not here.

ORLANDO

What, would you have me beg for my food? Or become a lowlife, sticking up travelers on the road? This is all that's left for me to do, but I won't do it. I'd rather give myself up to the hatred of a violent brother who refuses to recognize that we are brothers.

ADAM

But don't do that. I have five-hundred gold coins, which I carefully saved when I was working for your late father. I meant to use it for my retirement, to help me when my old body was lame and forgotten in some dark corner. But take the money, and God, who feeds even the raven and looks after even the sparrow, will comfort me in my old age. Here is the gold, I give it all to you. Let me be your servant. I know I may be old, but I'm strong and healthy, because in my youth I never drank nor lived recklessly. Therefore, my old age is like a blustery winter: cold, but kindly. Let me go with you. I'll do everything a younger man could do for you.

ORLANDO
> O good old man, how well in thee appears
> The constant service of the antique world,
> When service sweat for duty, not for meed.
> 60 Thou art not for the fashion of these times,
> Where none will sweat but for promotion,
> And having that do choke their service up
> Even with the having. It is not so with thee.
> But, poor old man, thou prun'st a rotten tree
> 65 That cannot so much as a blossom yield
> In lieu of all thy pains and husbandry.
> But come thy ways. We'll go along together,
> And ere we have thy youthful wages spent,
> We'll light upon some settled low content.

ADAM
> 70 Master, go on, and I will follow thee
> To the last gasp, with truth and loyalty.
> From seventeen years till now almost fourscore
> Here livèd I, but now live here no more.
> At seventeen years, many their fortunes seek,
> 75 But at fourscore, it is too late a week.
> Yet fortune cannot recompense me better
> Than to die well, and not my master's debtor.

Exeunt

ORLANDO

Oh, good old man, you're a great example of that old
work ethic, where people worked because it was their
duty, not just for the money. Your approach isn't the
fashion these days, when no one works hard except for
a promotion, and, as soon as they've got it, they stop
working. But in working for me, old man, you are
pruning a rotten tree: despite all your pains and
efforts, it won't yield a single blossom. Come along,
though. We'll go together, and before we've spent all
the savings of your youth, we'll find a way to make a
living.

ADAM

Go on, master, and I will follow you—with truth and
loyalty to my last breath. From the time I was seventeen, over sixty years ago, I have lived in this house,
but now I will live here no more. Many men seek their
fortune at seventeen; at eighty, it's a bit late. But fortune could not reward me better than to let me die
well, without owing my master anything.

They exit.

ACT 2, SCENE 4

Enter ROSALIND *for Ganymede,* CELIA *for Aliena, and*
TOUCHSTONE

ROSALIND
O Jupiter, how weary are my spirits!

TOUCHSTONE
I care not for my spirits, if my legs were not weary.

ROSALIND
I could find in my heart to disgrace my man's apparel and
to cry like a woman, but I must comfort the weaker vessel,
as doublet and hose ought to show itself courageous to
petticoat. Therefore courage, good Aliena.

CELIA
I pray you bear with me. I cannot go no further.

TOUCHSTONE
For my part, I had rather bear with you than bear you. Yet
I should bear no cross if I did bear you, for I think you have
no money in your purse.

ROSALIND
Well, this is the Forest of Arden.

TOUCHSTONE
Ay, now am I in Arden, the more fool I. When I was at home
I was in a better place, but travelers must be content.

ROSALIND
Ay, be so, good Touchstone.

Enter CORIN *and* SILVIUS

Look you who comes here, a young man and an old in
solemn talk.

ACT 2, SCENE 4

ROSALIND *(dressed as Ganymede)*, CELIA *(dressed as Aliena), and* TOUCHSTONE *enter.*

ROSALIND

Oh Lord, my spirits are tired!

TOUCHSTONE

I wouldn't care about my spirits, if my legs weren't tired.

ROSALIND

I'd insult my manly wardrobe by weeping like a woman if I didn't have to comfort the weaker vessel here, as the jacket and hose ought to be brave for the sake of the petticoat. So, have courage, good Aliena.

Doublet (jacket) and hose (heavy, pants-length stockings) were traditional men's clothing.

CELIA

Please bear with me. I can't go any further.

TOUCHSTONE

By "bear you," Touchstone means "carry you."

Elizabethan coins had crosses stamped on them.

I'd rather bear with you than bear you. But if I did carry you, it would be no cross to bear, because I'm pretty sure you don't have any money.

ROSALIND

Well, this is the Forest of Arden.

TOUCHSTONE

Yes, now I'm in Arden, and that makes me the bigger fool. When I was at home, I was in a better place. But travelers have to be content.

ROSALIND

Yes, be content, good Touchstone.

CORIN *and* SILVIUS *enter.*

Look who's coming: a young man and an old man, having a serious talk.

CORIN

That is the way to make her scorn you still.

SILVIUS

O Corin, that thou knew'st how I do love her!

CORIN

I partly guess, for I have loved ere now.

SILVIUS

20   No, Corin, being old, thou canst not guess,
Though in thy youth thou wast as true a lover
As ever sighed upon a midnight pillow.
But if thy love were ever like to mine—
As sure I think did never man love so—
25   How many actions most ridiculous
Hast thou been drawn to by thy fantasy?

CORIN

Into a thousand that I have forgotten.

SILVIUS

Oh, thou didst then ne'er love so heartily.
If thou rememb'rest not the slightest folly
30   That ever love did make thee run into,
Thou hast not loved.
Or if thou hast not sat as I do now,
Wearying thy hearer in thy mistress's praise,
Thou hast not loved.
35   Or if thou hast not broke from company
Abruptly, as my passion now makes me,
Thou hast not loved.
O Phoebe, Phoebe, Phoebe!

Exit

ROSALIND

Alas, poor shepherd, searching of thy wound,
40   I have by hard adventure found mine own.

CORIN

What you're doing is the way to make her scorn you continually.

SILVIUS

Oh, Corin, I wish you could understand how much I love her!

CORIN

I'm sure I can guess. I have been in love too, you know.

SILVIUS

No Corin, since you're old, you cannot guess—even if you were as dedicated a lover in your youth as there ever was, sighing and mooning all night long. If your love was anything like mine—and I'm sure that no man has loved as I love now—exactly how many ridiculous actions did your fantasizing lead you to?

CORIN

Oh, a thousand of them, all of which I've forgotten.

SILVIUS

Oh, then you never loved as wholeheartedly as me. If you can't remember the stupidest little thing love made you do, you haven't loved. Or if you haven't sat as I do now, boring your listener with all your lover's virtues, then you haven't loved. Or if you haven't broken away from human company, as my feelings now lead me to do, you haven't loved. O Phoebe, Phoebe, Phoebe!

He exits.

ROSALIND

Oh, poor shepherd! Listening to you speak of your wounded heart reminds me of my own pain.

TOUCHSTONE
And I mine. I remember when I was in love I broke my
sword upon a stone and bid him take that for coming a-
night to Jane Smile. And I remember the kissing of her
batler, and the cow's dugs that her pretty chopped hands
had milked. And I remember the wooing of a peascod
instead of her, from whom I took two cods and, giving her
them again, said with weeping tears, "Wear these for my
sake." We that are true lovers run into strange capers. But
as all is mortal in nature, so is all nature in love mortal in
folly.

ROSALIND
Thou speak'st wiser than thou art ware of.

TOUCHSTONE
Nay, I shall ne'er be ware of mine own wit till I break my
shins against it.

ROSALIND
Jove, Jove, this shepherd's passion
Is much upon my fashion.

TOUCHSTONE
And mine, but it grows something stale with me.

CELIA
I pray you, one of you question yond man, if he for gold will
give us any food. I faint almost to death.

TOUCHSTONE
(to CORIN*)* Holla, you clown!

ROSALIND
Peace, fool. He's not thy kinsman.

CORIN
Who calls?

TOUCHSTONE
Your betters, sir.

CORIN
Else are they very wretched.

TOUCHSTONE

Me too. I remember when I was in love, I broke my sword on a stone, and told him to take that for coming at night to see Jane Smile. I remember kissing her washing stick and the cow's udders that her pretty, chapped hands had milked. I remember wooing a pea plant in her name, and then taking two pea pods and begging her to wear them "for my sake." Those of us who are really in love will do the strangest things. But everything that lives is mortal, including the foolishness of love.

ROSALIND

You speak more wisely than you know.

TOUCHSTONE

Nah, I'll never be aware of my own wit, until I break my shins on it.

ROSALIND

By God! This shepherd's condition is like my own.

TOUCHSTONE

And like mine, but I'm getting a little tired of it.

CELIA

Please, one of you go ask that man over there if we can buy some food off him. I'm faint with hunger.

TOUCHSTONE

(to CORIN*)* Hey, clown!

ROSALIND

Shut up, fool. He's not your relative.

CORIN

Who's calling?

TOUCHSTONE

Your superiors.

CORIN

If they weren't my betters, they'd be pretty wretched indeed.

ROSALIND
Peace, I say. —Good even to you, friend.

CORIN
65   And to you, gentle sir, and to you all.

ROSALIND
I prithee, shepherd, if that love or gold
Can in this desert place buy entertainment,
Bring us where we may rest ourselves and feed.
Here's a young maid with travel much oppressed,
70   And faints for succor.

CORIN
Fair sir, I pity her
And wish, for her sake more than for mine own,
My fortunes were more able to relieve her.
But I am shepherd to another man
75   And do not shear the fleeces that I graze.
My master is of churlish disposition
And little recks to find the way to heaven
By doing deeds of hospitality.
Besides, his cote, his flocks, and bounds of feed
80   Are now on sale, and at our sheepcote now,
By reason of his absence, there is nothing
That you will feed on. But what is, come see,
And in my voice most welcome shall you be.

ROSALIND
What is he that shall buy his flock and pasture?

CORIN
85   That young swain that you saw here but erewhile,
That little cares for buying anything.

ROSALIND
I pray thee, if it stand with honesty,
Buy thou the cottage, pasture, and the flock,
And thou shalt have to pay for it of us.

ROSALIND

(to TOUCHSTONE) Stop it, I say.—Good evening to you, friend.

CORIN

Good evening to you, too, noble sir, and to all of you.

ROSALIND

Please sir, if love or money can buy anything in this empty place, tell us where we can rest and feed ourselves. We'll pay you for the information. We have a young woman here who is very tired from traveling and faint with hunger.

CORIN

Dear sir, I pity the lady and wish—more for her sake than my own—that I was more able to help her. But I'm a hired hand: I don't profit from the flocks I tend. My master is a brutish man and doesn't care much if he gets to heaven by deeds of hospitality or not. Besides, his cottage, his flocks, and his grazing rights are on sale now, and since he's not there, there's nothing to eat at our house. But let's see what's on hand. If I have anything to say about it, you will be most welcome there.

ROSALIND

Who wants to buy the flock and the pasture?

CORIN

That young man who was just here. But he doesn't really care about buying anything.

ROSALIND

Please, if you can do it without taking advantage of the young man, buy the cottage, pasture, and flock for us, and we'll pay you for it.

CELIA

90   And we will mend thy wages. I like this place,
        And willingly could waste my time in it.

CORIN

        Assuredly the thing is to be sold.
        Go with me. If you like upon report
        The soil, the profit, and this kind of life,
95   I will your very faithful feeder be
        And buy it with your gold right suddenly.

Exeunt

CELIA

And we will raise your wages. I like this place. I could see myself wasting time here.

CORIN

The thing is definitely going to be sold. Come with me. If you like what you see of the land, the profit that's possible, and this rustic life, I'll be your faithful servant, and buy the place with your gold right away.

They all exit.

ACT 2, SCENE 5

Enter AMIENS, JAQUES, *and others*

AMIENS
> *(sings)*
> *Under the greenwood tree*
> *Who loves to lie with me*
> *And turn his merry note*
> *Unto the sweet bird's throat,*
5 > *Come hither, come hither, come hither.*
> *Here shall he see*
> *No enemy*
> *But winter and rough weather.*

JAQUES
> More, more, I prithee, more.

AMIENS
10 > It will make you melancholy, Monsieur Jaques.

JAQUES
> I thank it. More, I prithee, more. I can suck melancholy out
> of a song as a weasel sucks eggs. More, I prithee, more.

AMIENS
> My voice is ragged. I know I cannot please you.

JAQUES
> I do not desire you to please me. I do desire you to sing.
15 > Come, more, another stanzo. Call you 'em "stanzos"?

AMIENS
> What you will, Monsieur Jaques.

JAQUES
> Nay, I care not for their names. They owe me nothing. Will
> you sing?

ACT 2, SCENE 5

AMIENS, JAQUES, *and others enter.*

AMIENS

(singing)
Whoever wants to lie with me,
Under the greenwood tree,
And turn his merry song
To follow the sweet bird's singing,
Come here, come here, come here.
Here you will find
No enemy
Besides winter and rough weather.

JAQUES

More, more, please, more.

AMIENS

It's only going to make you sad, Monsieur Jaques.

JAQUES

I'm glad about that. More, please, more. I can suck sadness out of a song the way a weasel sucks eggs. More, please, more.

AMIENS

My voice is ragged. I know I won't please you.

JAQUES

I don't want you to please me, I want you to sing. Come on, another stanza—is that what you call 'em, "stanzas"?

AMIENS

Call them whatever you want, Monsieur Jaques.

JAQUES

Nah, I don't care what their names are; they owe me nothing. Will you sing?

By "names," Jaques is thinking of the signatures on I.O.U notes, in which the name legally requires that the debt be honored.

AMIENS

More at your request than to please myself.

JAQUES

20   Well then, if ever I thank any man, I'll thank you. But that
they call "compliment" is like th' encounter of two dog-
apes. And when a man thanks me heartily, methinks I have
given him a penny and he renders me the beggarly thanks.
Come, sing. And you that will not, hold your tongues.

AMIENS

25   Well, I'll end the song.—Sirs, cover the while; the duke will
drink under this tree.—He hath been all this day to look
you.

JAQUES

And I have been all this day to avoid him. He is too
disputable for my company. I think of as many matters as
30   he, but I give heaven thanks and make no boast of them.
Come, warble, come.

EVERYONE

(singing)
Who doth ambition shun
And loves to live i' th' sun,
Seeking the food he eats
35   *And pleased with what he gets,*
Come hither, come hither, come hither.
Here shall he see
No enemy
But winter and rough weather.

JAQUES

40   I'll give you a verse to this note that I made yesterday in
despite of my invention.

AMIENS

Okay, but only because you want me to.

JAQUES

Well then, if I've ever thanked a man, I'll thank you now. But two men complimenting each other is like two baboons getting together. Whenever a man compliments me, I feel like he's a beggar and I just gave him a penny—an embarrassing exchange. Come on, sing—and those of you who won't sing, shut up.

AMIENS

Well, I'll finish the song I started.—Meanwhile, sirs, set the table. The duke will drink under this tree.— He's been looking for you all day, you know.

JAQUES

And I've been avoiding him all day. He's too argumentative for me. I think of as many things as he does, but I just thank heaven and don't show off about it. Come, warble for me.

EVERYONE

(singing)
Whoever shuns ambition
And loves to live in the sun,
Hunting the food he eats
Pleased with what he finds,
Come here, come here, come here.
Here he will find
No enemy
But winter and rough weather.

JAQUES

I wrote a verse to this tune, though it's not very imaginative. I'll give it you.

AMIENS
And I'll sing it. *(taking paper from* JAQUES*)* Thus it goes:
If it do come to pass
That any man turn ass,
45   *Leaving his wealth and ease*
A stubborn will to please,
Ducdame, ducdame, ducdame.
Here shall he see
Gross fools as he,
50   *An if he will come to me.*

AMIENS
What's that "ducdame"?

JAQUES
'Tis a Greek invocation, to call fools into a circle. I'll go
sleep if I can. If I cannot, I'll rail against all the first-born of
Egypt.

AMIENS
55   And I'll go seek the duke. His banquet is prepared.

Exeunt severally

AMIENS

And I'll sing it. *(taking a paper from* JAQUES*)* It goes like this:
(sings)
If it should come to pass
That any man turns into an ass
And leaves his wealth and ease
Simply to please his stubborn will
Ducdame, ducdame, ducdame.
Here he will see
Fools as stupid as he
If he will only come to me.

AMIENS

What's that word "ducdame"?

The actual meaning of "ducdame" is heavily debated. Jaques's answer seems to be mainly a jab at the noblemen who have followed Duke Senior into the woods.

JAQUES

It's a Greek invocation, calling fools into a circle. I'm going to take a nap, if I can—if I can't, I'll curse all the first-born children of Egypt.

AMIENS

And I'll go find the duke; his banquet is ready.

They all exit in separate directions.

ACT 2, SCENE 6

Enter ORLANDO *and* ADAM

ADAM
Dear master, I can go no further. Oh, I die for food. Here lie
I down and measure out my grave. Farewell, kind master.

ORLANDO
Why, how now, Adam? No greater heart in thee? Live a
little, comfort a little, cheer thyself a little. If this uncouth
5   forest yield anything savage, I will either be food for it or
bring it for food to thee. Thy conceit is nearer death than thy
powers. For my sake, be comfortable. Hold death awhile at
the arm's end. I will here be with thee presently, and if I
bring thee not something to eat, I will give thee leave to die.
10 But if thou diest before I come, thou art a mocker of my
labor. Well said. Thou look'st cheerly, and I'll be with thee
quickly. Yet thou liest in the bleak air. Come, I will bear thee
to some shelter, and thou shalt not die for lack of a dinner
if there live anything in this desert. Cheerly, good Adam.

Exeunt

ACT 2, SCENE 6

ORLANDO *and* ADAM *enter.*

ADAM

Dear master, I can't go any farther. Oh, I'm dying of hunger. I'll lie down here and measure out my grave. Farewell, kind master.

ORLANDO

Hey, what's this, Adam? No braver than this? Live a little, be comforted a little, cheer up a little. If I can find any animal in this wild forest, I'll either be food for it or bring it as food for you. You're not as close to death as you think you are. For my sake, make yourself comfortable; keep death at arm's length for a while. I'll be back soon, and if I haven't brought you anything to eat, I will give you permission to die. But if you die before I return, you'll have made a mockery of my efforts. There we go! You look happier already, and I'll be back quickly. But you're lying out in the cold. Come, I'll carry you to shelter. And you won't die for lack of dinner, if there's anything at all to eat in this desert-like forest. Cheer up, good Adam.

They exit.

ACT 2, SCENE 7

Enter DUKE SENIOR, AMIENS, *and* LORDS *like outlaws.*

DUKE SENIOR
I think he be transformed into a beast,
For I can nowhere find him like a man.

FIRST LORD
My lord, he is but even now gone hence.
Here was he merry, hearing of a song.

DUKE SENIOR
5   If he, compact of jars, grow musical,
We shall have shortly discord in the spheres.
Go seek him. Tell him I would speak with him.

Enter JAQUES

FIRST LORD
He saves my labor by his own approach.

DUKE SENIOR
Why, how now, monsieur? What a life is this
10   That your poor friends must woo your company?
What, you look merrily.

JAQUES
A fool, a fool, I met a fool i' th' forest,
A motley fool. A miserable world!
As I do live by food, I met a fool,
15   Who laid him down and basked him in the sun
And railed on Lady Fortune in good terms,
In good set terms, and yet a motley fool.
"Good morrow, fool," quoth I. "No, sir," quoth he,
"Call me not 'fool' till heaven hath sent me fortune."

ACT 2, SCENE 7

DUKE SENIOR, AMIENS, *and* LORDS *enter, dressed like outlaws.*

DUKE SENIOR

I think he must have turned into an animal, because I can't find him anywhere looking like a man.

FIRST LORD

My lord, he just left here. He was happy here, listening to a song.

DUKE SENIOR

If that man, who's made up of conflicts, becomes musical, then there must be something wrong with the universe. Go find him. Tell him I want to speak with him.

JAQUES *enters.*

FIRST LORD

He saved me the trouble: here he comes.

DUKE SENIOR

Well, what's going on, mister? What kind of life do you lead that your poor friends must beg for your company? What, you look amused.

JAQUES

Fools were conventionally distinguished by their motley (multicolored) costume

A fool, a fool! I met a fool in the forest, wearing motley. What a miserable world! As sure as I eat to stay alive, I met a fool who was lying in the sun and complaining about his fortune. He spoke smartly, though he was a fool. "Good morning, fool," I said. "No, sir," he said, "don't call me a fool until heaven has sent me my fortune."

Proverbially, Fortune is supposed to favor fools.

20   And then he drew a dial from his poke
      And, looking on it with lackluster eye,
      Says very wisely, "It is ten o'clock.
      Thus we may see," quoth he, "how the world wags.
      'Tis but an hour ago since it was nine,
25   And after one hour more 'twill be eleven.
      And so from hour to hour we ripe and ripe,
      And then from hour to hour we rot and rot,
      The motley fool thus moral on the time,
      And thereby hangs a tale." When I did hear
30   My lungs began to crow like chanticleer
      That fools should be so deep-contemplative,
      And I did laugh sans intermission
      An hour by his dial. O noble fool!
      A worthy fool! Motley's the only wear.

DUKE SENIOR
35   What fool is this?

JAQUES
      O worthy fool!—One that hath been a courtier
      And says, "If ladies be but young and fair,
      They have the gift to know it." And in his brain,
      Which is as dry as the remainder biscuit
40   After a voyage, he hath strange places crammed
      With observation, the which he vents
      In mangled forms. Oh, that I were a fool!
      I am ambitious for a motley coat.

DUKE SENIOR
      Thou shalt have one.

Then he pulled a watch from his bag and, looking at it solemnly, said, "It's ten o'clock. This way, we can see how the world moves. Only an hour ago it was nine, and in another hour it will be eleven. And so, from hour to hour we ripen, and from hour to hour we rot. And there's a story behind that." When I heard that motley fool moralizing on the subject of time, I began to crow like a rooster. Hearing a fool speaking so contemplatively made me laugh non-stop for an hour. Oh, noble fool! A worthy fool! Motley is the only thing to wear.

DUKE SENIOR

Who is this fool?

JAQUES

In Shakespeare's time, people thought different brains, with different amounts of moisture, processed information differently. A "dry" brain took a long time to be "impressed" by information

A worthy fool! He's been a courtier and says, "If ladies are young and pretty, they always know it." His brain is dry as a sailor's biscuit and crammed with all sorts of strange observations, which he presents in mangled fashion. Oh, I wish I were a fool! I'm ambitious for one of those motley coats.

DUKE SENIOR

You shall have one.

JAQUES

45   It is my only suit,
     Provided that you weed your better judgments
     Of all opinion that grows rank in them
     That I am wise. I must have liberty
     Withal, as large a charter as the wind,
50   To blow on whom I please, for so fools have.
     And they that are most gallèd with my folly,
     They most must laugh. And why, sir, must they so?
     The "why" is plain as way to parish church:
     He that a fool doth very wisely hit
55   Doth very foolishly, although he smart,
     Not to seem senseless of the bob. If not,
     The wise man's folly is anatomized
     Even by the squand'ring glances of the fool.
     Invest me in my motley. Give me leave
60   To speak my mind, and I will through and through
     Cleanse the foul body of th' infected world,
     If they will patiently receive my medicine.

DUKE SENIOR

     Fie on thee! I can tell what thou wouldst do.

JAQUES

     What, for a counter, would I do but good?

DUKE SENIOR

65   Most mischievous foul sin in chiding sin,
     For thou thyself hast been a libertine,
     As sensual as the brutish sting itself,
     And all th' embossèd sores and headed evils
     That thou with license of free foot hast caught
70   Wouldst thou disgorge into the general world.

JAQUES

     Why, who cries out on pride
     That can therein tax any private party?
     Doth it not flow as hugely as the sea
     Till that the weary very means do ebb?

JAQUES

That's all I ask from you, as long as you promise to rid
yourself of any rotten idea that I am wise. Like the
wind, I must have the freedom to blast anyone I
please, as fools do. And whoever is most irritated by
my foolishness has to laugh the hardest. Why, sir,
must he? Well, it's as plain as the beaten path to a par-
ish church. Any person who thinks I'm satirizing
them would be stupid if they didn't pretend not to be
hurt by my joke. Otherwise, they'd be admitting I was
talking about them, and the fool would expose the
wise man's foolishness with a joke that wasn't even
meant for him. Dress me up in motley. Let me speak
my mind, and I'll rid the world of its sickness—if it
will only tolerate my medicine.

DUKE SENIOR

To hell with you! I know what you'd do.

JAQUES

What would I do besides good?

DUKE SENIOR

You would be committing a wicked sin by chiding
other people for sinning, because you yourself have
been a terrible sinner, as carnal in your appetites as
lust itself, and all the swollen pustules of sin that you
acquired in your freedom you now want to burst and
shoot back into the world at large.

JAQUES

But if I cry out against pride in general, how can anyone say I'm accusing a particular person? Aren't we
talking about a problem as vast as the sea, that keeps
flowing until all the wealth in the world is almost used
up by everyone showing off?

75   What woman in the city do I name,
      When that I say the city-woman bears
      The cost of princes on unworthy shoulders?
      Who can come in and say that I mean her,
      When such a one as she such is her neighbor?
80   Or what is he of basest function
      That says his bravery is not of my cost,
      Thinking that I mean him, but therein suits
      His folly to the mettle of my speech?
      There then. How then, what then? Let me see wherein
85   My tongue hath wronged him. If it do him right,
      Then he hath wronged himself. If he be free,
      Why then my taxing like a wild goose flies
      Unclaimed of any man. But who comes here?

      Enter ORLANDO, *with his sword drawn*

ORLANDO
      Forbear, and eat no more.

JAQUES
90   Why, I have eat none yet.

ORLANDO
      Nor shalt not till necessity be served.

JAQUES
      Of what kind should this cock come of?

DUKE SENIOR
      Art thou thus boldened, man, by thy distress
      Or else a rude despiser of good manners,
95   That in civility thou seem'st so empty?

ORLANDO
      You touched my vein at first. The thorny point
      Of bare distress hath ta'en from me the show
      Of smooth civility, yet am I inland bred
      And know some nurture. But forbear, I say.
100   He dies that touches any of this fruit
      Till I and my affairs are answerèd.

What woman in the city am I talking about when I say that the clothes on a city-woman's unworthy back are rich enough to suit a prince? Who can say I mean just her when all her neighbors are exactly like her? And when some lowlife protests that *his* fancy clothes aren't my problem, isn't he basically admitting that I'm talking about him? Well, then. Tell me how I've wronged him. If I was right about him, he's the one who's done wrong. If he isn't guilty of the faults I'm talking about, well then, my accusations fly by like wild geese, whom no one owns, since they don't apply to any man. But who is this?

ORLANDO *enters with his sword drawn.*

ORLANDO

Stop, and eat no more.

JAQUES

But I haven't eaten anything yet.

ORLANDO

And you won't until the needy eat.

JAQUES

What kind of fighting cock is this?

DUKE SENIOR

Are you acting so boldly from hardship or because you despise good manners? Why do you seem so lacking in civility?

ORLANDO

You were right the first time. My piercing distress has stripped me of smooth manners. But I wasn't raised in the forest, and I was somewhat well-bred. But stop, I say. Whoever eats this fruit before I've been taken care of dies.

JAQUES
> An you will not be answered with reason, I must die.

DUKE SENIOR
> What would you have? Your gentleness shall force
> More than your force move us to gentleness.

ORLANDO
105   I almost die for food, and let me have it.

DUKE SENIOR
> Sit down and feed, and welcome to our table.

ORLANDO
> Speak you so gently? Pardon me, I pray you.
> I thought that all things had been savage here,
> And therefore put I on the countenance
110   Of stern commandment. But whate'er you are
> That in this desert inaccessible,
> Under the shade of melancholy boughs,
> Lose and neglect the creeping hours of time,
> If ever you have looked on better days,
115   If ever been where bells have knolled to church,
> If ever sat at any good man's feast,
> If ever from your eyelids wiped a tear
> And know what 'tis to pity and be pitied,
> Let gentleness my strong enforcement be,
120   In the which hope I blush and hide my sword.

DUKE SENIOR
> True is it that we have seen better days
> And have with holy bell been knolled to church,
> And sat at good men's feasts and wiped our eyes
> Of drops that sacred pity hath engendered.
125   And therefore sit you down in gentleness,
> And take upon command what help we have
> That to your wanting may be ministered.

JAQUES

If you won't listen to reason, I'll have to die.

DUKE SENIOR

What would you like? Gentlemanly manners have more sway around here than force does.

ORLANDO

I'm dying for food, so let me have some.

DUKE SENIOR

Sit down and eat, and welcome to our table.

ORLANDO

Do you really speak like such a gentleman? I beg your pardon. I thought everything out here was wild, which is why I acted so stern and commanding. But whoever you are—you who sit in the dark shade, losing track of time in this remote forest—if you have ever seen better days or been to church or sat at a man's table for a feast or wiped a tear from your eye, if you know what it is to pity and be pitied, let my kindness and nobility persuade you. With that hope, I'll blush at my rudeness and put away my sword.

DUKE SENIOR

We have in fact seen better days and been summoned to church by the ringing of the holy bell and sat at good men's feasts and cried tears of pity—therefore, sit down and take whatever will satisfy your needs.

ORLANDO
Then but forbear your food a little while
Whiles, like a doe, I go to find my fawn
130 And give it food. There is an old poor man
Who after me hath many a weary step
Limped in pure love. Till he be first sufficed,
Oppressed with two weak evils, age and hunger,
I will not touch a bit.

DUKE SENIOR
135 Go find him out,
And we will nothing waste till you return.

ORLANDO
I thank you; and be blessed for your good comfort.

Exit

DUKE SENIOR
Thou seest we are not all alone unhappy.
This wide and universal theater
140 Presents more woeful pageants than the scene
Wherein we play in.

JAQUES
All the world's a stage,
And all the men and women merely players.
They have their exits and their entrances,
145 And one man in his time plays many parts,
His acts being seven ages. At first the infant,
Mewling and puking in the nurse's arms.
Then the whining schoolboy with his satchel
And shining morning face, creeping like snail
150 Unwillingly to school. And then the lover,
Sighing like furnace, with a woeful ballad
Made to his mistress' eyebrow. Then a soldier,
Full of strange oaths and bearded like the pard,
Jealous in honor, sudden and quick in quarrel,

ORLANDO

Then please, put off your eating for a little while I, like a mother doe, find my fawn and bring it food. There is a poor old man who, purely out of love, has limped after me for miles. He's burdened by two debilitating evils—age and hunger. Until he's fed, I won't eat a thing.

DUKE SENIOR

Go find him. We won't touch a thing till you return.

ORLANDO

Thank you, and God bless you for your hospitality.

He exits.

DUKE SENIOR

You see, we're not alone in our unhappiness. This wide, universal theater has more sad plays than our own little scene.

JAQUES

The whole world is a stage, and all the men and women merely actors. They have their exits and their entrances, and in his lifetime a man will play many parts, his life separated into seven acts. In the first act he is an infant, whimpering and puking in his nurse's arms. Then he's the whining schoolboy, with a book bag and a bright, young face, creeping like a snail unwillingly to school. Then he becomes a lover, huffing and puffing like a furnace as he writes sad poems about his mistress's eyebrows. In the fourth act, he's a soldier, full of foreign curses, with a beard like a panther, eager to defend his honor and quick to fight.

155 Seeking the bubble reputation
Even in the cannon's mouth. And then the justice,
In fair round belly with good capon lined,
With eyes severe and beard of formal cut,
Full of wise saws and modern instances;
160 And so he plays his part. The sixth age shifts
Into the lean and slippered pantaloon
With spectacles on nose and pouch on side,
His youthful hose, well saved, a world too wide
For his shrunk shank, and his big manly voice,
165 Turning again toward childish treble, pipes
And whistles in his sound. Last scene of all,
That ends this strange eventful history,
Is second childishness and mere oblivion,
Sans teeth, sans eyes, sans taste, sans everything.

Enter ORLANDO *bearing* ADAM

DUKE SENIOR
170 Welcome. Set down your venerable burden,
And let him feed.

ORLANDO
I thank you most for him.

ADAM
So had you need.—
I scarce can speak to thank you for myself.

DUKE SENIOR
175 Welcome. Fall to. I will not trouble you
As yet to question you about your fortunes.—
Give us some music, and, good cousin, sing.

On the battlefield, he puts himself in front of the cannon's mouth, risking his life to seek fame that is as fleeting as a soap bubble. In the fifth act, he is a judge, with a nice fat belly from all the bribes he's taken. His eyes are stern, and he's given his beard a respectable cut. He's full of wise sayings and up-to-the-minute anecdotes: that's the way he plays his part. In the sixth act, the curtain rises on a skinny old man in slippers, glasses on his nose and a money bag at his side. The stockings he wore in his youth hang loosely on his shriveled legs now, and his bellowing voice has shrunk back down to a childish squeak. In the last scene of our play—the end of this strange, eventful history—our hero, full of forgetfulness, enters his second childhood: without teeth, without eyes, without taste, without everything.

ORLANDO *enters carrying* ADAM.

DUKE SENIOR

Welcome. Set the honorable old man down and let him eat.

ORLANDO

I thank you very much on his behalf.

ADAM

You had better do that. I can barely speak to thank you myself.

DUKE SENIOR

Welcome. Eat. I won't trouble you yet with questions about your situation.—Some music, please, and, good friend, sing.

AMIENS
(sings)
Blow, blow, thou winter wind.
Thou art not so unkind
180 *As man's ingratitude.*
Thy tooth is not so keen,
Because thou art not seen,
Although thy breath be rude.
Heigh-ho, sing heigh-ho, unto the green holly.
185 *Most friendship is feigning, most loving mere folly.*
Then heigh-ho, the holly.
This life is most jolly.
Freeze, freeze, thou bitter sky,
That dost not bite so nigh
190 *As benefits forgot.*
Though thou the waters warp,
Thy sting is not so sharp
As friend remembered not.
Heigh-ho, sing heigh-ho, unto the green holly.
195 *Most friendship is feigning, most loving mere folly.*
Then heigh-ho, the holly.
This life is most jolly.

DUKE SENIOR
If that you were the good Sir Rowland's son,
As you have whispered faithfully you were,
200 And as mine eye doth his effigies witness
Most truly limned and living in your face,
Be truly welcome hither. I am the duke
That loved your father. The residue of your fortune
Go to my cave and tell me.—Good old man,
205 Thou art right welcome as thy master is.
Support him by the arm. Give me your hand,
And let me all your fortunes understand.

Exeunt

AMIENS

(singing)
Blow, blow, winter wind.
You aren't as harsh
As men's ingratitude.
Your teeth aren't as sharp,
As you are invisible,
Even though your breath is an assault.
Heigh-ho! Sing, heigh-ho! Sing to the green holly.
Most friendship is false, most love simply foolishness:
Then heigh-ho, to the holly.
This life is really jolly.
Freeze, freeze, you bitter sky,
Your bite isn't as painful
As when good deeds are forgotten.
Even though you can freeze water
Your sting is not as sharp
As the friend who is forgotten.
Heigh-ho! Sing, heigh-ho! Sing to the green holly.
Most friendship is false, most love simply foolishness.
Then heigh-ho, to the holly.
This life is really jolly.

DUKE SENIOR

If you really are Sir Rowland's son, as you've just
whispered to me—and I can absolutely see the like-
ness in your face— you are truly welcome here. I am
the duke who loved your father. Come to my cave and
tell me the rest of your story.—Good old man, you are
as welcome here as your master is. Give him your arm.
Give me your hand, and explain your situation to me.

They all exit.

ACT THREE

SCENE 1

Enter DUKE FREDERICK, LORDS, *and* OLIVER

DUKE FREDERICK

Not see him since? Sir, sir, that cannot be.
But were I not the better part made mercy,
I should not seek an absent argument
Of my revenge, thou present. But look to it:

5   Find out thy brother, wheresoe'er he is.
Seek him with candle. Bring him, dead or living,
Within this twelvemonth or turn thou no more
To seek a living in our territory.
Thy lands and all things that thou dost call thine

10 Worth seizure, do we seize into our hands
Till thou canst quit thee by thy brother's mouth
Of what we think against thee.

OLIVER

Oh, that your Highness knew my heart in this:
I never loved my brother in my life.

DUKE FREDERICK

15 More villain thou.—Well, push him out of doors
And let my officers of such a nature
Make an extent upon his house and lands.
Do this expediently, and turn him going.

Exeunt

ACT THREE

SCENE 1

DUKE FREDERICK *enters, with lords and* OLIVER.

DUKE FREDERICK
> You haven't seen him since? Sir, sir, that can't be true.
> If I weren't a merciful man, I'd forget about your
> missing brother and punish you in his place. But do
> this: find your brother, wherever he is. Bring him here
> dead or alive within the next year, or get out off my
> land. I'm seizing your lands and all that you possess
> until your brother gives testimony that absolves you
> of any guilt.

OLIVER
> I wish your Highness knew my true feelings in this
> matter: I have never in my life loved my brother.

DUKE FREDERICK
> That makes you an even bigger villain.—Well, throw
> him out, and have my officers seize his house and
> lands. Do this immediately, and send him packing.

They all exit.

ACT 3, SCENE 2

Enter ORLANDO, *with a paper*

ORLANDO

    Hang there, my verse, in witness of my love.
    And thou, thrice-crownéd queen of night, survey
    With thy chaste eye, from thy pale sphere above,
    Thy huntress' name that my full life doth sway.
5   O Rosalind, these trees shall be my books,
    And in their barks my thoughts I'll character,
    That every eye which in this forest looks
    Shall see thy virtue witnessed everywhere.
    Run, run, Orlando, carve on every tree
10   The fair, the chaste, and unexpressive she.

Exit

Enter CORIN *and* TOUCHSTONE

CORIN

    And how like you this shepherd's life, Master Touchstone?

TOUCHSTONE

    Truly, shepherd, in respect of itself, it is a good life; but in
    respect that it is a shepherd's life, it is naught. In respect
    that it is solitary, I like it very well; but in respect that it is
15   private, it is a very vile life. Now in respect it is in the fields,
    it pleaseth me well; but in respect it is not in the court, it is
    tedious. As it is a spare life, look you, it fits my humor well;
    but as there is no more plenty in it, it goes much against my
    stomach. Hast any philosophy in thee, shepherd?

ACT 3, SCENE 2

ORLANDO *enters, holding a piece of paper.*

ORLANDO

Hang there on this tree, you lines of poetry, and bear witness to my love. And you, goddess of the moon, queen of the night—with your chaste eye, from your pale home up above—watch your huntress, who has the power to control my life. Oh, Rosalind, these trees will be my books—I'll write my thoughts down on their bark. That way, everyone who passes through this forest will find your virtues everywhere. Run, run, Orlando, on every tree carve praises of her beauty, her virtue, and her inexpressibility.

He exits.

CORIN *and* TOUCHSTONE *enter.*

CORIN

And how are you liking the shepherd's life, Master Touchstone?

TOUCHSTONE

Well, in and of itself, it is a good life, but given that it's a shepherd's life, it's worthless. In the fact that it's solitary, I enjoy it very much; but in the sense that it's private, it's terrible. Now, I'm very pleased with it being outdoors, but in its not being at the court, it is boring. Being a simple life, it suits me very well, but being a life without plenty, it doesn't suit me at all. Are you any kind of philosopher yourself, shepherd?

Diana—in Greek and Roman mythology, goddess of the moon and the hunt—was the patron of virgin maidens like Rosalind.

CORIN

20   No more but that I know the more one sickens, the worse at
        ease he is, and that he that wants money, means, and
        content is without three good friends; that the property of
        rain is to wet, and fire to burn; that good pasture makes fat
        sheep; and that a great cause of the night is lack of the sun;
25   that he that hath learned no wit by nature nor art may
        complain of good breeding or comes of a very dull kindred.

TOUCHSTONE

        Such a one is a natural philosopher. Wast ever in court,
        shepherd?

CORIN

        No, truly.

TOUCHSTONE

30   Then thou art damned.

CORIN

        Nay, I hope.

TOUCHSTONE

        Truly, thou art damned, like an ill-roasted egg, all on one
        side.

CORIN

        For not being at court? Your reason.

TOUCHSTONE

35   Why, if thou never wast at court, thou never saw'st good
        manners; if thou never saw'st good manners, then thy
        manners must be wicked, and wickedness is sin, and sin is
        damnation. Thou art in a parlous state, shepherd.

CORIN

Only in that I know that the sicker one gets, the worse one feels, and that the man who lacks money, employment, and happiness is without three good friends. I know that rain makes things wet and fire burns things. I know that a good pasture makes sheep fat, that the main cause of night is the absence of sun, and that the man who isn't smart by nature and hasn't learned anything from his schooling will complain of his lack of good manners, or he comes from very dull parents indeed.

TOUCHSTONE

You're a natural-born philosopher! Were you ever at court, shepherd?

CORIN

Honestly, no.

TOUCHSTONE

Then you are damned.

CORIN

I hope not.

TOUCHSTONE

Eggs were roasted in ashes and had to be rotated frequently to avoid burning. Yep, you're damned like a roasted egg: all on one side.

CORIN

I'm damned for not having been at court? Explain.

TOUCHSTONE

Well, if you were never at court, you were never exposed to good manners; if you never witnessed good manners, your manners must be wicked; wickedness is a sin, and committing sins leads to damnation. You are in a perilous state, shepherd.

CORIN

Not a whit, Touchstone. Those that are good manners at
40   the court are as ridiculous in the country as the behavior of
the country is most mockable at the court. You told me you
salute not at the court but you kiss your hands. That
courtesy would be uncleanly if courtiers were shepherds.

TOUCHSTONE

Instance, briefly. Come, instance.

CORIN

45   Why, we are still handling our ewes, and their fells, you
know, are greasy.

TOUCHSTONE

Why, do not your courtier's hands sweat? And is not the
grease of a mutton as wholesome as the sweat of a man?
Shallow, shallow. A better instance, I say. Come.

CORIN

50   Besides, our hands are hard.

TOUCHSTONE

Your lips will feel them the sooner. Shallow again. A more
sounder instance. Come.

CORIN

And they are often tarred over with the surgery of our
sheep; and would you have us kiss tar? The courtier's hands
55   are perfumed with civet.

TOUCHSTONE

Most shallow man. Thou worms' meat in respect of a good
piece of flesh, indeed. Learn of the wise and perpend: civet
is of a baser birth than tar, the very uncleanly flux of a cat.
Mend the instance, shepherd.

CORIN

60   You have too courtly a wit for me. I'll rest.

CORIN

Not at all, Touchstone. The good manners of the court look as silly in the country as country behavior is laughable at the court. You told me that you don't salute at the court but kiss hands. Now, if courtiers were shepherds, that kind of courtesy would be unclean.

TOUCHSTONE

Give a quick example. Come, explain.

CORIN

Why, because we're always handling our ewes, and their fleece, as you know, is greasy.

TOUCHSTONE

What, don't courtiers' hands sweat? And isn't a sheep's grease as wholesome as a man's sweat? That's a poor example. A better example—come on.

CORIN

Besides, our hands are hard and calloused.

TOUCHSTONE

Then your lips will feel them more quickly. Shallow thinking, yet again. Come on.

CORIN

Sheep wounds were treated with tar.

Our hands are often covered in tar, from performing surgery on our sheep. Would you have us country folks kiss each other's tarred hands? Courtiers' hands are perfumed.

TOUCHSTONE

You shallow thinker! You worthless man! You are about as much of a thinker as worm's meat is a nice steak. Learn from the wise, and comprehend: the courtier's perfume is made from cat discharge—much more disgusting than tar. Fix your example, shepherd.

CORIN

Your wit is too courtly for me. I'll rest now.

TOUCHSTONE
Wilt thou rest damned? God help thee, shallow man. God
make incision in thee; thou art raw.

CORIN
Sir, I am a true laborer. I earn that I eat, get that I wear, owe
no man hate, envy no man's happiness, glad of other men's
65   good, content with my harm, and the greatest of my pride
is to see my ewes graze and my lambs suck.

TOUCHSTONE
That is another simple sin in you, to bring the ewes and the
rams together and to offer to get your living by the
copulation of cattle; to be bawd to a bellwether and to
70   betray a she-lamb of a twelvemonth to a crooked-pated old
cuckoldly ram, out of all reasonable match. If thou be'st not
damned for this, the devil himself will have no shepherds.
I cannot see else how thou shouldst 'scape.

CORIN
Here comes young Master Ganymede, my new mistress's
75   brother.

Enter ROSALIND, *with a paper, reading*

ROSALIND
(as Ganymede, reading)
From the east to western Ind,
No jewel is like Rosalind.
Her worth being mounted on the wind,
Through all the world bears Rosalind.
80   All the pictures fairest lined
Are but black to Rosalind.
Let no fair be kept in mind
But the fair of Rosalind.

TOUCHSTONE

You're going to rest while you're still damned? God help you, foolish man. Pray God does some surgery on you: you need to be fixed .

CORIN

Sir, I'm a true, simple laborer: I earn what I eat, get what I wear, hate no man, envy no man's happiness, am happy for other men's good fortune and satisfied with my own bad fortune, and the source of my greatest pride is watching my ewes graze and my lambs feed.

TOUCHSTONE

That's another sin arising from your ignorance: you bring ewes and rams together and make your living by their copulation. You act as a pimp to a young ewe by forcing her to have sex with a crooked-headed, horny old ram—a totally unreasonable match. If you're not damned for that, then the devil must be keeping shepherds out of hell; I can't see how else you can hope to escape.

CORIN

Here comes young Mr. Ganymede, my new mistress's brother.

ROSALIND enters, reading from a sheet of paper.

ROSALIND

(reading, as Ganymede)
From the far east to the west Indies
There is no jewel like Rosalind.
Her worth is carried on the wind
And it blows throughout the world, carrying the name of Rosalind.
All the most beautiful paintings
Are black when compared to Rosalind.
Don't think of any beauty
But the beauty of Rosalind.

TOUCHSTONE

I'll rhyme you so eight years together, dinners and suppers
and sleeping hours excepted. It is the right butter-women's
rank to market.

ROSALIND

Out, fool.

TOUCHSTONE

For a taste:
If a hart do lack a hind,
Let him seek out Rosalind.
If the cat will after kind,
So, be sure, will Rosalind.
Winter garments must be lined,
So must slender Rosalind.
They that reap must sheaf and bind,
Then to cart with Rosalind.
Sweetest nut hath sourest rind;
Such a nut is Rosalind.
He that sweetest rose will find
Must find love's prick, and Rosalind.
This is the very false gallop of verses. Why do you infect
yourself with them?

ROSALIND

Peace, you dull fool. I found them on a tree.

TOUCHSTONE

Truly, the tree yields bad fruit.

ROSALIND

I'll graft it with you, and then I shall graft it with a medlar.
Then it will be the earliest fruit i' th' country, for you'll be
rotten ere you be half ripe, and that's the right virtue of the
medlar.

TOUCHSTONE

I could rhyme like that for eight years in a row, excepting meal times and sleeping hours. That awful, plodding rhyme sounded like a row of dairy women stomping off to market.

ROSALIND

Oh, stop, fool.

TOUCHSTONE

Let me try:
If there's a buck who needs a doe
Tell him Rosalind will do.
A cat in heat will look for a mate,
And Rosalind certainly will too.
Winter garments need to be filled with something,
And so does skinny Rosalind.
After you harvest, you have to sheaf and bind
So throw ripe Rosalind on the harvest cart.
The sweetest nut has the sourest rind
And Rosalind is that kind of nut.
The man who finds the sweetest rose
Will be pricked by it, and by Rosalind.
This is exactly the false way that verses gallop along. Why bother with them?

ROSALIND

Quiet, you stupid fool. I found them on a tree.

TOUCHSTONE

Well, the tree bears rotten fruit.

ROSALIND

I'll graft you onto that tree, and when I do I'll be grafting onto it a medlar. The fruit the tree bears will be the earliest to ripen in the country because, God knows, *you'll* be rotten before you're half-ripe, which is how medlars are.

In other words, Touchstone will be "rotten," or decomposing in his grave, before he's "ripe," or wise. Medlar fruits were eaten when they were rotten.

TOUCHSTONE

You have said, but whether wisely or no, let the forest
110   judge.

Enter CELIA, *with a writing*

ROSALIND

Peace. Here comes my sister reading. Stand aside.

CELIA

(as Aliena, reads) Why should this a desert be?
For it is unpeopled? No.
Tongues I'll hang on every tree
115   That shall civil sayings show.
Some how brief the life of man
Runs his erring pilgrimage,
That the stretching of a span
Buckles in his sum of age;
120   Some of violated vows
'Twixt the souls of friend and friend.
But upon the fairest boughs,
Or at every sentence end,
Will I "Rosalinda" write,
125   Teaching all that read to know
The quintessence of every sprite
Heaven would in little show.
Therefore heaven nature charged
That one body should be filled
130   With all graces wide-enlarged.
Nature presently distilled
Helen's cheek, but not her heart,
Cleopatra's majesty,
Atalanta's better part,
135   Sad Lucretia's modesty.

TOUCHSTONE

All right, you've had your say, but we'll let the forest judge whether or not you spoke wisely.

CELIA *enters with a piece of paper.*

ROSALIND

Quiet! Here comes my cousin, reading something; step aside.

CELIA

(reading, as Aliena) Why should this place be a desert
Just because there are no people in it? No,
I'll hang these poems on every tree,
And they will voice the thoughts of a city.
Some will be about how man's brief life
is spent in wandering,
his entire life contained
in the width of an open hand.
Some poems will be about betrayals
Committed by friends.
But on the prettiest branches
Or at the end of every sentence
I'll write "Rosalinda,"
Teaching everyone who can read
that the essence of every spirit
Is contained in this one woman.
Heaven commanded Nature
To fill her one body
With all the graces that women contain.
Nature took
Helen's beautiful face, but not her fickle heart;
Cleopatra's majesty,
The best of Atalanta,
And unhappy Lucretia's modesty.

Helen, Cleopatra, Atalanta, and Lucretia are beautiful women featured in Greek and Roman mythology.

Thus Rosalind of many parts
By heavenly synod was devised,
Of many faces, eyes, and hearts
To have the touches dearest prized.
140   Heaven would that she these gifts should have
And I to live and die her slave.

ROSALIND
O most gentle Jupiter, what tedious homily of love have
you wearied your parishioners withal, and never cried,
"Have patience, good people."

CELIA
145   *(as Aliena)* How now?—Back, friends.—Shepherd, go off a
little.—Go with him, sirrah.

TOUCHSTONE
Come, shepherd, let us make an honorable retreat, though
not with bag and baggage, yet with scrip and scrippage.

Exeunt CORIN *and* TOUCHSTONE

CELIA
Didst thou hear these verses?

ROSALIND
150   Oh, yes, I heard them all, and more too, for some of them
had in them more feet than the verses would bear.

CELIA
That's no matter. The feet might bear the verses.

ROSALIND
Ay, but the feet were lame and could not bear themselves
without the verse, and therefore stood lamely in the verse.

So, by heaven's decree, Rosalind
Was composed
Of different faces, eyes, and hearts,
so that she might have the most prized touches of all.
Heaven wanted Rosalind to have these gifts
And me to live and die,as her slave.

ROSALIND

Oh, Lord—what tedious sayings about love have you
been wearing out your congregation with? Shouldn't
you have warned, "Be patient, good people"?

CELIA

What are you saying?—Shoo, Shepherd, go a little
ways away.—Go with him, Touchstone.

TOUCHSTONE

Come on, shepherd, let's make an honorable retreat,
though not with all the trappings of a full army; just
with a shepherd's pouch and the stuff he puts in it.

CORIN *and* TOUCHSTONE *exit.*

CELIA

Were you listening to these verses?

ROSALIND

bear = carry

Each verse of poetry is supposed to have only a certain number of "feet," or accented syllables. Bad poets, like Orlando, cram their lines with too many words.

Oh yes, I heard them all, and more, too. Some of those
lines had more feet than the verses could bear.

CELIA

That's not a problem: the feet can bear the verses.

ROSALIND

Rosalind is making fun of the poor quality of Orlando's poetry.

Sure, but these feet were lame, and couldn't have
stood up without the support of the verses. They
stood lamely in the verse.

CELIA

155   But didst thou hear without wondering how thy name
        should be hanged and carved upon these trees?

ROSALIND

        I was seven of the nine days out of the wonder before you
        came, for look here what I found on a palm tree. I was never
        so berhymed since Pythagoras' time, that I was an Irish rat,
160   which I can hardly remember.

CELIA

        Trow you who hath done this?

ROSALIND

        Is it a man?

CELIA

        And a chain, that you once wore, about his neck. Change
        you color?

ROSALIND

165   I prithee, who?

CELIA

        O Lord, Lord, it is a hard matter for friends to meet, but
        mountains may be removed with earthquakes and so
        encounter.

ROSALIND

        Nay, but who is it?

CELIA

170   Is it possible?

ROSALIND

        Nay, I prithee now, with most petitionary vehemence, tell
        me who it is.

CELIA

        O wonderful, wonderful, and most wonderful wonderful,
        and yet again wonderful, and after that, out of all
175   whooping!

CELIA

But did you listen to all that poetry without even wondering about what your name is doing on all these trees?

ROSALIND

In Ireland, poets aimed satirical verses at their enemies.

Supposedly, they killed rats by rhyming them to death.

I was working through my wonder when you arrived. Look at what I found on a palm tree. I haven't been rhymed about like this since my past life, when I was an Irish rat, but I can hardly remember that.

CELIA

Do you know who wrote these?

ROSALIND

Was it a man?

CELIA

And he had a chain that once belonged to you hanging around his neck. Are you blushing?

ROSALIND

Please, who?

CELIA

Oh God, God! It's difficult to bring two friends together, but even mountains can be moved together by earthquakes.

ROSALIND

No, who are you talking about?

CELIA

Is it possible?

ROSALIND

No, I'm begging you now, tell me who it is.

CELIA

Oh, this is wonderful, wonderful—just wonderful wonderful! And another wonderful, and beyond-my-ability-to-express wonderful!

ROSALIND

Good my complexion, dost thou think though I am
caparisoned like a man, I have a doublet and hose in my
disposition? One inch of delay more is a South Sea of
discovery. I prithee, tell me who is it quickly, and speak
180   apace. I would thou couldst stammer, that thou might'st
pour this concealed man out of thy mouth as wine comes
out of a narrow-mouthed bottle—either too much at once,
or none at all. I prithee take the cork out of thy mouth, that
I may drink thy tidings.

CELIA

185   So you may put a man in your belly.

ROSALIND

Is he of God's making? What manner of man? Is his head
worth a hat or his chin worth a beard?

CELIA

Nay, he hath but a little beard.

ROSALIND

Why, God will send more, if the man will be thankful. Let
190   me stay the growth of his beard, if thou delay me not the
knowledge of his chin.

CELIA

It is young Orlando, that tripped up the wrestler's heels and
your heart both in an instant.

ROSALIND

Nay, but the devil take mocking. Speak sad brow and true
195   maid.

CELIA

I' faith, coz, 'tis he.

ROSALIND

Orlando?

CELIA

Orlando.

ROSALIND

> Good grief, do you think that just because I'm dressed like a man, I have a man's patience? Every second you delay is as long and dull as a journey to South Seas. I'm begging you, tell me who it is quickly, and speak fast. I wish you could just stammer this hidden man out of your mouth like wine out of a narrow-necked bottle: either too much at once or none at all. I'm begging you, take the cork out of your mouth so I can drink the news.

CELIA

> So you want to put a man in your belly.

ROSALIND

> Did God make him? I mean, what sort of man is he? Is he enough of a man to wear a hat and grow a beard?

CELIA

> No, he has only a little beard.

ROSALIND

> Well, eventually God will send him some more hair, if he thanks Him. I'll wait till his beard grows in, if you'll just hurry up and tell me what chin that beard is on.

CELIA

> It's Orlando, who triumphed over both the wrestler and you in the same instant.

ROSALIND

> Damn you for mocking me. Speak seriously and honestly.

CELIA

> Really, cousin, it's him.

ROSALIND

> Orlando?

CELIA

> Orlando.

ROSALIND

200

Alas the day, what shall I do with my doublet and hose? What did he when thou saw'st him? What said he? How looked he? Wherein went he? What makes him here? Did he ask for me? Where remains he? How parted he with thee? And when shalt thou see him again? Answer me in one word.

CELIA

205

You must borrow me Gargantua's mouth first. 'Tis a word too great for any mouth of this age's size. To say ay and no to these particulars is more than to answer in a catechism.

ROSALIND

But doth he know that I am in this forest and in man's apparel? Looks he as freshly as he did the day he wrestled?

CELIA

210

It is as easy to count atomies as to resolve the propositions of a lover. But take a taste of my finding him, and relish it with good observance. I found him under a tree like a dropped acorn.

ROSALIND

215

It may well be called Jove's tree when it drops forth such fruit.

CELIA

Give me audience, good madam.

ROSALIND

Proceed.

CELIA

There lay he, stretched along like a wounded knight.

ROSALIND

220

Though it be pity to see such a sight, it well becomes the ground.

ROSALIND

"In a word" means "quickly," but Celia teasingly takes Rosalind literally —"in *one* word."

Oh no! What am I going to do in my man's clothing? What did he do when you saw him? What did he say? How did he look? Where did he go? What brings him here? Did he ask about me? Where is he staying? How did he say good-bye? And when will you see him again? Answer me in a word.

CELIA

Gargantua was a giant with an enormous appetite for food and drink featured in *Gargantua and Pantagruel*, by the late-medieval writer Rabelais.

You'd better get me Gargantua's mouth first. The word's too big for any mouth nowadays. Answering "yes" and "no" to all those questions would be harder than answering a catechism.

A catechism is a summary of a religious doctrine, often in the form of questions and answers.

ROSALIND

But does he know that I'm here in the forest and dressed in men's clothing? Does he look as bright and handsome as the day we saw him wrestling?

CELIA

It's easier to count specks than to answer a lover's millions of questions. But taste my story, and relish it by paying attention. I found Orlando under a tree, like a dropped acorn.

ROSALIND

That tree could be called God's tree, since it drops such wonderful fruit.

CELIA

Let me talk, good lady.

ROSALIND

Go on.

CELIA

He lay there, stretched out like a wounded knight.

ROSALIND

Though that must have been a pitiful sight, the ground looked beautiful.

CELIA

Cry "holla" to thy tongue, I prithee. It curvets
unseasonably. He was furnished like a hunter.

ROSALIND

Oh, ominous! He comes to kill my heart.

CELIA

225   I would sing my song without a burden. Thou bring'st me
out of tune.

ROSALIND

Do you not know I am a woman? When I think, I must
speak. Sweet, say on.

CELIA

You bring me out. Soft, comes he not here?

Enter ORLANDO *and* JAQUES

ROSALIND

'Tis he. Slink by, and note him.

JAQUES

230   I thank you for your company, but, good faith, I had as lief
have been myself alone.

ORLANDO

And so had I, but yet, for fashion sake, I thank you too for
your society.

JAQUES

God be wi' you. Let's meet as little as we can.

ORLANDO

235   I do desire we may be better strangers.

JAQUES

I pray you mar no more trees with writing love songs in
their barks.

ORLANDO

I pray you mar no more of my verses with reading them ill-
favoredly.

CELIA

Cry, "whoa!" to your tongue, please. It's leaping about like a frisky horse. He was dressed like a hunter.

ROSALIND

Oh, that's ominous! He has come to kill my heart.

CELIA

I'd like to sing my song solo. You're making me go off-key.

ROSALIND

Don't you know that I'm a woman? Whatever I think, I have to say. Sweetheart, go on.

CELIA

You've made me lose the tune. Quiet! Isn't that him heading this way?

ORLANDO *and* JAQUES *enter.*

ROSALIND

That's him. Let's slink off, and watch him from a hiding place.

JAQUES

Thanks for your company but, really, I would have preferred being alone.

ORLANDO

Me too, but still, for the sake of good manners, I'll say thanks for your company.

JAQUES

Goodbye. Let's meet as little as we can.

ORLANDO

I also hope that we can be better strangers.

JAQUES

Please don't ruin any more trees by carving love poems on their barks.

ORLANDO

Please don't ruin any more of my poems by reading them so badly.

JAQUES

240   Rosalind is your love's name?

ORLANDO

Yes, just.

JAQUES

I do not like her name.

ORLANDO

There was no thought of pleasing you when she was
christened.

JAQUES

245   What stature is she of?

ORLANDO

Just as high as my heart.

JAQUES

You are full of pretty answers. Have you not been
acquainted with goldsmiths' wives and conned them out of
rings?

ORLANDO

250   Not so. But I answer you right painted cloth, from whence
you have studied your questions.

JAQUES

You have a nimble wit. I think 'twas made of Atalanta's
heels. Will you sit down with me? And we two will rail
against our mistress the world and all our misery.

ORLANDO

255   I will chide no breather in the world but myself, against
whom I know most faults.

JAQUES

The worst fault you have is to be in love.

ORLANDO

'Tis a fault I will not change for your best virtue. I am weary
of you.

JAQUES

Your love's name is Rosalind?

ORLANDO

Yes, that's it.

JAQUES

I don't like her name.

ORLANDO

They weren't looking to please you when they christened her.

JAQUES

How tall is she?

ORLANDO

Just as tall as my heart.

JAQUES

Gold rings were often inscribed with lines from trite love poems.

You're sure full of smooth answers. Are you friendly with goldsmiths' wives, and memorized your little speeches off of their rings?

ORLANDO

Painted cloths were sometimes hung in place of tapestries and featured trite, moralistic sayings.

No, but I can answer you just like those painted cloths, where I suppose you memorized all your questions.

JAQUES

The mythical Atalanta was a very fast runner.

You have a quick wit; I think it must be made out of Atalanta's heels. Why don't you sit down with me? The two of us can complain about our mistress—the world—and all our miseries.

ORLANDO

I won't blame anyone in this world but myself, whose faults I'm most familiar with.

JAQUES

Your worst fault is being in love.

ORLANDO

Well, it's a fault I wouldn't trade for your best virtue. I'm tired of you.

JAQUES

260   By my troth, I was seeking for a fool when I found you.

ORLANDO

He is drowned in the brook. Look but in, and you shall see
him.

JAQUES

There I shall see mine own figure.

ORLANDO

Which I take to be either a fool or a cipher.

JAQUES

265   I'll tarry no longer with you. Farewell, good Signior Love.

ORLANDO

I am glad of your departure. Adieu, good Monsieur
Melancholy.

Exit JAQUES

ROSALIND

(aside to CELIA*)* I will speak to him like a saucy lackey, and
under that habit play the knave with him.—Do you hear,
270   forester?

ORLANDO

Very well. What would you?

ROSALIND

(as Ganymede) I pray you, what is 't o'clock?

ORLANDO

You should ask me what time o' day. There's no clock in the
forest.

ROSALIND

275   Then there is no true lover in the forest, else sighing every
minute and groaning every hour would detect the lazy foot
of time as well as a clock.

JAQUES

Well, I *was* looking for a fool when I found you, so I suppose I shouldn't be surprised.

ORLANDO

He's drowned in the brook: look in, and you'll see him.

JAQUES

There I'll see only myself.

ORLANDO

Which is either a fool or a nothing.

JAQUES

I'm not going to waste any more time with you. Good-bye, good Mr. Love.

ORLANDO

I'm glad to see you go. Adieu, good Mr. Depression.

JAQUES exits.

ROSALIND

(speaking so that only CELIA can hear) I'm going to talk to him like I'm an insolent boy, so I can play a trick on him.—Can you hear me, forester?

ORLANDO

Very well. What do you want?

ROSALIND

(as Ganymede) Please, what's the hour?

ORLANDO

You should ask me what time of day it is, instead. There's no clock here in the forest.

ROSALIND

Then there must be no lovers in the forest, either, because they're as good as a clock, marking the lazy foot of time with a sigh every minute and a groan every hour.

ORLANDO
> And why not the swift foot of time? Had not that been as
> proper?

ROSALIND
280 > By no means, sir. Time travels in diverse paces with diverse
> persons. I'll tell you who time ambles withal, who time
> trots withal, who time gallops withal, and who he stands
> still withal.

ORLANDO
> I prithee, who doth he trot withal?

ROSALIND
285 > Marry, he trots hard with a young maid between the
> contract of her marriage and the day it is solemnized. If the
> interim be but a se'nnight, time's pace is so hard that it
> seems the length of seven year.

ORLANDO
> Who ambles time withal?

ROSALIND
290 > With a priest that lacks Latin and a rich man that hath not
> the gout, for the one sleeps easily because he cannot study
> and the other lives merrily because he feels no pain—the
> one lacking the burden of lean and wasteful learning, the
> other knowing no burden of heavy tedious penury. These
295 > time ambles withal.

ORLANDO
> Who doth he gallop withal?

ROSALIND
> With a thief to the gallows, for though he go as softly as foot
> can fall, he thinks himself too soon there.

ORLANDO
> Who stays it still withal?

ROSALIND
300 > With lawyers in the vacation, for they sleep between term
> and term, and then they perceive not how time moves.

ORLANDO

Why didn't you say "the swift steps" of time instead of the "lazy foot"? Wouldn't that have been just as appropriate?

ROSALIND

No, not at all, sir. Time travels at different speeds for different people. I can tell you who time strolls for, who it trots for, who it gallops for, and who it stops cold for.

ORLANDO

Okay, who does it trot for?

ROSALIND

Well, it trots for a young woman between the time she gets engaged and the time she marries: the time that's passed may only be a week, but it always feels like seven years.

ORLANDO

Who does time amble for?

ROSALIND

For a priest who doesn't know his Latin or a rich man who is free from the gout. The one sleeps easily because he isn't up late studying and the other lives merrily because he's free from pain. The first lacks the burden of intense, exhausting study, and the second is spared the burden of heavy, exhausting poverty. Time ambles for both men.

ORLANDO

Who does it gallop for?

ROSALIND

For a thief on his way to the gallows. Such a man walks as slowly as possible and, even so, gets there too soon.

ORLANDO

Who does it stand still for?

ROSALIND

For lawyers on vacation, because they sleep their holidays away, with no sense of how time moves.

ORLANDO
Where dwell you, pretty youth?

ROSALIND
With this shepherdess, my sister, here in the skirts of the
forest like fringe upon a petticoat.

ORLANDO
305   Are you native of this place?

ROSALIND
As the cony that you see dwell where she is kindled.

ORLANDO
Your accent is something finer than you could purchase in
so removed a dwelling.

ROSALIND
I have been told so of many. But indeed an old religious
310   uncle of mine taught me to speak, who was in his youth an
inland man, one that knew courtship too well, for there he
fell in love. I have heard him read many lectures against it,
and I thank God I am not a woman, to be touched with so
many giddy offenses as he hath generally taxed their whole
315   sex withal.

ORLANDO
Can you remember any of the principal evils that he laid to
the charge of women?

ROSALIND
There were none principal. They were all like one another
as half-pence are, every one fault seeming monstrous till his
320   fellow fault came to match it.

ORLANDO
I prithee, recount some of them.

ORLANDO

Where do you live, pretty young man?

ROSALIND

With this shepherdess, my sister, on the outskirts of the forest. We live like fringe on the edges of a petticoat.

ORLANDO

Were you born here?

ROSALIND

Just like the rabbit, who lives where she is born.

ORLANDO

Your speech is more refined than I would expect in such a remote place as this.

ROSALIND

Many people have told me so. Actually, an old religious uncle of mine taught me how to speak, and he was brought up in the city. He knew too much about courtship, because he fell in love back there, and when he came here he constantly lectured against it. Thank God I'm not a woman and afflicted with all the giddiness that troubles that entire sex.

ORLANDO

What were the primary evils he claimed women were guilty of?

ROSALIND

There were no primary ones. All of women's faults are as alike as one half-pence is to another. Each of a woman's faults seems monstrous until you're presented with the next one, which is just as bad.

ORLANDO

Please, tell me some of them.

ROSALIND
No, I will not cast away my physic but on those that are sick.
There is a man haunts the forest that abuses our young
plants with carving "Rosalind" on their barks, hangs odes
325 upon hawthorns and elegies on brambles, all, forsooth,
deifying the name of Rosalind. If I could meet that fancy-
monger I would give him some good counsel, for he seems
to have the quotidian of love upon him.

ORLANDO
I am he that is so love-shaked. I pray you tell me your
330 remedy.

ROSALIND
There is none of my uncle's marks upon you. He taught me
how to know a man in love, in which cage of rushes I am
sure you are not prisoner.

ORLANDO
What were his marks?

ROSALIND
335 A lean cheek, which you have not; a blue eye and sunken,
which you have not; an unquestionable spirit, which you
have not; a beard neglected, which you have not—but I
pardon you for that, for simply your having in beard is a
younger brother's revenue. Then your hose should be
340 ungartered, your bonnet unbanded, your sleeve
unbuttoned, your shoe untied, and everything about you
demonstrating a careless desolation. But you are no such
man. You are rather point-device in your accouterments, as
loving yourself than seeming the lover of any other.

ORLANDO
345 Fair youth, I would I could make thee believe I love.

ROSALIND

No, I won't give my medicine away to anyone but the sick. There's a man haunting this forest who abuses the trees by carving "Rosalind" on their barks. He hangs his odes on the hawthorns and his elegies on the brambles—each of these poems praising to the heavens one "Rosalind." Now if I could find this man, this dream-catcher, I would give him some good advice, because he is truly love-sick.

ORLANDO

Well, I'm the man you're speaking of. Please, tell me your cure.

ROSALIND

But you don't have any of the symptoms my uncle told me about. He taught me how to recognize a man in love, and you're not a prisoner of love, I'm sure.

ORLANDO

What did he say the symptoms were?

ROSALIND

A thin face, which you don't have; a sleepless, sunken eye, which you don't have; an irritable temper, which you don't have; a neglected beard, which you don't have—but that might not be so telling, since you don't have much beard anyway. Your stockings should be falling down around your ankles, your hat flying off your head, your sleeves unbuttoned, your shoes untied, and everything about you demonstrating carelessness and misery. But you're no such man. You're so neat and well put-together that you look like you love yourself more than anyone else.

ORLANDO

Young boy, I wish I could make you believe that I'm in love.

ROSALIND

Me believe it? You may as soon make her that you love believe it, which I warrant she is apter to do than to confess she does. That is one of the points in the which women still give the lie to their consciences. But, in good sooth, are you he that hangs the verses on the trees wherein Rosalind is so admired?

ORLANDO

I swear to thee, youth, by the white hand of Rosalind, I am that he, that unfortunate he.

ROSALIND

But are you so much in love as your rhymes speak?

ORLANDO

Neither rhyme nor reason can express how much.

ROSALIND

Love is merely a madness and, I tell you, deserves as well a dark house and a whip as madmen do, and the reason why they are not so punished and cured is that the lunacy is so ordinary that the whippers are in love, too. Yet I profess curing it by counsel.

ORLANDO

Did you ever cure any so?

ROSALIND

Make me believe it? You might as well make the one you love believe it, which she's more likely to do than admit that she does—that's one of the ways that women fool their own consciences. But really, are you the one who's been hanging on the trees those poems that speak so admiringly of Rosalind?

ORLANDO

I swear to you by Rosalind's own pretty hand that I am that unfortunate man.

ROSALIND

Are you really as in love as your poems declare?

ORLANDO

Neither rhyme nor reason can express how much I love her.

ROSALIND

Love is merely a form of insanity, and I tell you, lovers deserve the nuthouse just like crazy people do. The only reason they don't get punished and cured is that the disease is so commonplace that the nuthouse nurses are usually suffering from it, too. But I promise it can be cured with some guidance.

ORLANDO

Have you ever cured anyone this way before?

ROSALIND
Yes, one, and in this manner. He was to imagine me his
love, his mistress, and I set him every day to woo me; at
which time would I, being but a moonish youth, grieve, be
365 effeminate, changeable, longing and liking, proud,
fantastical, apish, shallow, inconstant, full of tears, full of
smiles; for every passion something, and for no passion
truly anything, as boys and women are, for the most part,
cattle of this color; would now like him, now loathe him;
370 then entertain him, then forswear him; now weep for him,
then spit at him, that I drave my suitor from his mad humor
of love to a living humor of madness, which was to forswear
the full stream of the world and to live in a nook merely
monastic. And thus I cured him, and this way will I take
375 upon me to wash your liver as clean as a sound sheep's
heart, that there shall not be one spot of love in 't.

ORLANDO
I would not be cured, youth.

ROSALIND
I would cure you if you would but call me Rosalind and
come every day to my cote and woo me.

ORLANDO
380 Now, by the faith of my love, I will. Tell me where it is.

ROSALIND
Go with me to it, and I'll show it you; and by the way you
shall tell me where in the forest you live. Will you go?

ORLANDO
With all my heart, good youth.

ROSALIND
Nay, you must call me Rosalind.—Come, sister, will you
385 go?

Exeunt

ROSALIND

Yes, one, and this is how I did it. He had to imagine that I was the girl he was in love with. I made him woo me every day. When he did, being the changeable boy I am, I'd mope, act effeminate, switch moods, long for him, like him, be proud and standoffish, be dreamy, full of mannerisms, unpredictable, full of tears and then smiles; be passionate about everything, then nothing. Most boys and women act just like this. I'd like him one minute and despise him the next; cry for him, then spit at him—until finally I drove love out and anger in. He abandoned the world, and hid himself away in a monastery. So I cured him, and I'll cure you just the same, leaving you as clean as a sheep's heart, without one spot of love in you.

ORLANDO

I don't want to be cured, boy.

ROSALIND

I could cure you, if you just called me Rosalind and came by my cottage every day to woo me.

ORLANDO

By my faith in love, I will, then. Tell me where you live.

ROSALIND

Come with me, I'll show you, and along the way, you can tell me where you live. Will you come?

ORLANDO

Wholeheartedly, good young man.

ROSALIND

No, you have to call me Rosalind.—Sister, you're coming?

They all exit.

ACT 3, SCENE 3

Enter TOUCHSTONE *and* AUDREY, *and* JAQUES *behind*

TOUCHSTONE
Come apace, good Audrey. I will fetch up your goats,
Audrey. And how, Audrey? Am I the man yet? Doth my
simple feature content you?

AUDREY
Your features, Lord warrant us! What features?

TOUCHSTONE
5   I am here with thee and thy goats, as the most capricious
poet, honest Ovid, was among the Goths.

JAQUES
(aside) O knowledge ill-inhabited, worse than Jove in a
thatched house.

TOUCHSTONE
When a man's verses cannot be understood nor a man's
10   good wit seconded with the forward child, understanding,
it strikes a man more dead than a great reckoning in a little
room. Truly, I would the gods had made thee poetical.

AUDREY
I do not know what "poetical" is. Is it honest in deed and
word? Is it a true thing?

TOUCHSTONE
15   No, truly, for the truest poetry is the most feigning, and
lovers are given to poetry, and what they swear in poetry
may be said as lovers they do feign.

AUDREY
Do you wish then that the gods had made me poetical?

TOUCHSTONE
I do, truly, for thou swear'st to me thou art honest. Now, if
20   thou wert a poet, I might have some hope thou didst feign.

ACT 3, SCENE 3

TOUCHSTONE *and* AUDREY *enter, with* JAQUES *following unseen.*

TOUCHSTONE

Come on, sweet Audrey. I'll get your goats, Audrey. Well now, what do you think, Audrey? Am I the man for you, Audrey? Do my simple features please you?

AUDREY

Your features, God help us! What features?

TOUCHSTONE

Goths sounds like *goats.* Touchstone makes a series of puns, none of which Audrey catches.

Well, I'm out here with you and your goats, in the same way that the witty poet Ovid was abandoned to the barbaric Goths.

JAQUES

(to himself) Oh, knowledge put to such bad use is worse than a god cooped up in a hut.

TOUCHSTONE

When a man's jokes fall that flat, it's as depressing as getting a large bill for a short stay in a little room. Really, Audrey, I wish you were more poetical.

AUDREY

I don't know what "poetical" means. Is it "chaste in word and action"? Does it mean being truthful?

TOUCHSTONE

Not really, for the truest poetry is often the most artificial. Lovers are fond of poetry and often concoct great lies in their poems.

AUDREY

But you still wish the gods had made me poetical?

TOUCHSTONE

I do, in fact. Right now you swear to me that you are a virgin; if you were a poet, I might have some hope you were lying.

AUDREY

Would you not have me honest?

TOUCHSTONE

No, truly, unless thou wert hard-favored, for honesty
coupled to beauty is to have honey a sauce to sugar.

JAQUES

(aside) A material fool.

AUDREY

25 Well, I am not fair, and therefore I pray the gods make me
honest.

TOUCHSTONE

Truly, and to cast away honesty upon a foul slut were to put
good meat into an unclean dish.

AUDREY

I am not a slut, though I thank the gods I am foul.

TOUCHSTONE

30 Well, praised be the gods for thy foulness; sluttishness may
come hereafter. But be it as it may be, I will marry thee; and
to that end I have been with Sir Oliver Martext, the vicar of
the next village, who hath promised to meet me in this place
of the forest and to couple us.

JAQUES

35 *(aside)* I would fain see this meeting.

AUDREY

Well, the gods give us joy.

TOUCHSTONE

Amen. A man may, if he were of a fearful heart, stagger in
this attempt, for here we have no temple but the wood, no
assembly but horn-beasts. But what though? Courage. As
40 horns are odious, they are necessary. It is said, "Many a
man knows no end of his goods." Right: many a man has
good horns and knows no end of them.

AUDREY

What, you don't want me to be chaste?

TOUCHSTONE

Not really, unless you were ugly. Chastity and beauty together in one woman is like sweetening sugar with honey.

JAQUES

(to himself) A sensible fool.

AUDREY

Well, I'm not beautiful, so I hope that I can at least be chaste.

TOUCHSTONE

Yes, but wasting chastity on a dirty slut is like putting good meat in a dirty dish.

AUDREY

I'm not a slut—I keep myself clean—but I thank God I am ugly.

TOUCHSTONE

Well, praise the Lord you're ugly. Maybe sluttishness will follow. Be that as it may, I'm going to marry you. To that end, I've spoken with Sir Oliver Martext, the vicar from the next village, and he's promised to meet us here and marry us.

JAQUES

(to himself) This I'd like to see.

AUDREY

Well, God bless this marriage!

TOUCHSTONE

Amen. You know, some men, who have fear in their hearts, might falter at this point. After all, these woods aren't a proper church, and there's no congregation here but horned animals. But who cares? I'll be brave. Horns may be hateful, but they're also necessary. They say, "Many a man doesn't know the full extent of what he owns." Exactly: many a man will see no end to the horns his wife furnishes him with.

Men whose wives cheated on them (called cuckolds) were imagined as having horns. Touchstone plays on the connection between a deer's horns and a cuckold's horns.

Well, that is the dowry of his wife; 'tis none of his own
getting. Horns? Even so. Poor men alone? No, no. The
45   noblest deer hath them as huge as the rascal. Is the single
man therefore blessed? No. As a walled town is more
worthier than a village, so is the forehead of a married man
more honorable than the bare brow of a bachelor. And by
how much defense is better than no skill, by so much is a
50   horn more precious than to want.

Enter SIR OLIVER MARTEXT

Here comes Sir Oliver.—Sir Oliver Martext, you are well
met. Will you dispatch us here under this tree, or shall we
go with you to your chapel?

SIR OLIVER MARTEXT
  Is there none here to give the woman?

TOUCHSTONE
55   I will not take her on gift of any man.

SIR OLIVER MARTEXT
  Truly, she must be given, or the marriage is not lawful.

JAQUES
  (advancing) Proceed, proceed. I'll give her.

TOUCHSTONE
  Good even, good Monsieur What-ye-call't. How do you,
sir? You are very well met. God 'ild you for your last
60   company. I am very glad to see you. Even a toy in hand here,
sir. Nay, pray be covered.

JAQUES
  Will you be married, motley?

Well, that's what the wife brings to the marriage. He didn't do anything to get them. Horns? Well, there they are. Only for poor men? No, no. The nobleman's are as huge as the underfed villager's. Is the single man lucky, then? No. Just as a town protected by a wall around it is worth more than a low-lying village, a married man's horned forehead is more honorable than a bachelor's bare forehead. Just as it's better to be skilled at self-defense than it is to avoid fighting, it's better to risk a horn by marrying. Here comes Sir Oliver.

SIR OLIVER MARTEXT *enters.*

Sir Oliver Martext, we're glad to see you. Will you marry us here, under this tree, or should we follow you to your chapel?

SIR OLIVER MARTEXT
Is there anyone to give the bride away?

TOUCHSTONE
I don't want to take another man's second-hand goods.

SIR OLIVER MARTEXT
No, someone has to give her away or the marriage isn't legal.

JAQUES
(coming forward) Go on, proceed—I'll give her away.

TOUCHSTONE
Good evening, Mr. What'shisname. How are you, sir? We're glad to see you. God bless you for being here. I'm very glad to see you. This is just a trifling matter here, sir. No, no, put your hat back on.

JAQUES
Do you want to get married, fool?

TOUCHSTONE

As the ox hath his bow, sir, the horse his curb, and the
falcon her bells, so man hath his desires; and as pigeons bill,
65   so wedlock would be nibbling.

JAQUES

And will you, being a man of your breeding, be married
under a bush like a beggar? Get you to church, and have a
good priest that can tell you what marriage is. This fellow
will but join you together as they join wainscot. Then one
70   of you will prove a shrunk panel and, like green timber,
warp, warp.

TOUCHSTONE

(aside) I am not in the mind but I were better to be married
of him than of another, for he is not like to marry me well,
and not being well married, it will be a good excuse for me
75   hereafter to leave my wife.

JAQUES

Go thou with me, and let me counsel thee.

TOUCHSTONE

Come, sweet Audrey. We must be married, or we must live
in bawdry.—Farewell, good Master Oliver, not
O sweet Oliver,
80   *O brave Oliver,*
Leave me not behind thee
But
Wind away,
Begone, I say,
85   *I will not to wedding with thee.*

Exeunt JAQUES, TOUCHSTONE, *and* AUDREY

SIR OLIVER MARTEXT

'Tis no matter. Ne'er a fantastical knave of them all shall
flout me out of my calling.

Exit

TOUCHSTONE

Just as the ox has his yoke, the horse its bridle, the falcon a tether, a man has his desires—to keep in check.

JAQUES

And, being a man of your breeding, you're going to be married under some shrubs like a beggar? Get yourself to a church and have a proper priest, who can tell you what marriage is all about, marry you. This man here will slap you two together like two pieces of wood panelling. Then one of you will warp and pull away— and there goes your marriage.

TOUCHSTONE

(to himself) I'd rather have this guy marry us, because he is not likely to marry us well, and if we're not married properly, I'll have a better excuse later to leave my wife.

JAQUES

Come with me and let me advise you.

TOUCHSTONE

Come, sweet Audrey. We have to be married properly. Otherwise, we'll be living in sin.—Goodbye, Sir Oliver. We're not singing,

Oh, sweet Oliver

Oh, sweet Oliver

Don't leave me behind—

but,

Go away, wind

Go, I say,

I'm not going to marry you.

Touchstone is singing a popular song of the day.

JAQUES, TOUCHSTONE, *and* AUDREY *exit.*

SIR OLIVER MARTEXT

It doesn't matter to me. None of these deranged rascals can shake me from my profession.

He exits.

ACT 3, SCENE 4

Enter ROSALIND *and* CELIA

ROSALIND
Never talk to me. I will weep.

CELIA
Do, I prithee, but yet have the grace to consider that tears
do not become a man.

ROSALIND
But have I not cause to weep?

CELIA
5   As good cause as one would desire. Therefore weep.

ROSALIND
His very hair is of the dissembling color.

CELIA
Something browner than Judas's. Marry, his kisses are
Judas's own children.

ROSALIND
I' faith, his hair is of a good color.

CELIA
10   An excellent color. Your chestnut was ever the only color.

ROSALIND
And his kissing is as full of sanctity as the touch of holy
bread.

CELIA
He hath bought a pair of cast lips of Diana. A nun of
winter's sisterhood kisses not more religiously. The very ice
15   of chastity is in them.

ROSALIND
But why did he swear he would come this morning, and
comes not?

ACT 3, SCENE 4

ROSALIND and CELIA enter.

ROSALIND

Don't talk to me. I'm going to cry.

CELIA

Go ahead if you want, but remember that crying doesn't suit a man.

ROSALIND

But don't I have good reason to cry?

CELIA

As good a reason as any. So go ahead and cry.

ROSALIND

Judas, the disciple who betrayed Jesus, was commonly depicted with red hair.

I mean, his hair is even red—the same color as that lying Judas.

CELIA

Judas betrayed Jesus to the Romans with a kiss.

No, it's a shade browner than Judas's—but his kisses are just like Judas's.

ROSALIND

No, really, his hair is a nice color.

CELIA

A very good color, this chestnut.

ROSALIND

His kiss is as holy as bread blessed by a priest.

CELIA

Diana was the patron goddess of virgins.

He must have bought a cast-iron pair of Diana's lips: an elderly nun isn't anymore devoted in her kissing than he is. His kiss is cold and chaste.

ROSALIND

But why would he promise to come visit me this morning and then not come?

CELIA
Nay, certainly, there is no truth in him.

ROSALIND
Do you think so?

CELIA
20   Yes, I think he is not a pick-purse nor a horse-stealer, but for his verity in love, I do think him as concave as a covered goblet or a worm-eaten nut.

ROSALIND
Not true in love?

CELIA
Yes, when he is in, but I think he is not in.

ROSALIND
25   You have heard him swear downright he was.

CELIA
"Was" is not "is." Besides, the oath of a lover is no stronger than the word of a tapster. They are both the confirmer of false reckonings. He attends here in the forest on the duke your father.

ROSALIND
30   I met the duke yesterday and had much question with him. He asked me of what parentage I was. I told him, of as good as he. So he laughed and let me go. But what talk we of fathers when there is such a man as Orlando?

CELIA
Oh, that's a brave man. He writes brave verses, speaks
35   brave words, swears brave oaths, and breaks them bravely, quite traverse, athwart the heart of his lover, as a puny tilter that spurs his horse but on one side breaks his staff like a noble goose; but all's brave that youth mounts and folly guides.

CELIA

Really, he's a total liar.

ROSALIND

Do you think so?

CELIA

Yes. He's not a pickpocket or a horse thief, but when it comes to truth in love, he's as hollow as a cup or a nut hollowed out by a worm.

ROSALIND

You think his feelings aren't true?

CELIA

Oh, I think they are—when he's in love. But he's not in love.

ROSALIND

But you heard him swear up and down that he was.

CELIA

He "was," but that doesn't mean he is anymore. Besides, the promises of a lover are as untrustworthy as a bartender handing you an inflated tab: they both swear to their lies. He's staying in the forest with your father now.

ROSALIND

I met my father in the woods yesterday and had a long conversation with him. He asked me who my parents were, and I told him they were as good as he was. He laughed at that and let me go. But why are we talking about my father, when a man like Orlando exists?

CELIA

This was considered a dishonorable move in jousting.

Oh, sure, he's a brave man! He writes brave poems, speaks brave words, makes brave promises, and then breaks them just as bravely. He's like a cowardly jouster, who breaks his lance across his opponent's shield, rather than directly against it. But everything's brave that a young man does and foolishness leads.

Enter CORIN

40   Who comes here?

CORIN
Mistress and master, you have oft inquired
After the shepherd that complained of love,
Who you saw sitting by me on the turf,
Praising the proud disdainful shepherdess
45   That was his mistress.

CELIA
(as Aliena) Well, and what of him?

CORIN
If you will see a pageant truly played
Between the pale complexion of true love
And the red glow of scorn and proud disdain,
50   Go hence a little, and I shall conduct you,
If you will mark it.

ROSALIND
(aside to CELIA*)* O, come, let us remove.
The sight of lovers feedeth those in love.
—*(as Ganymede)* Bring us to this sight, and you shall say
55   I'll prove a busy actor in their play.

Exeunt

CORIN *enters.*

Who's coming here?

CORIN

Mistress and master, you've often asked about that lovelorn shepherd you once saw me sitting with, the one who complained about the disdainful shepherdess he was in love with.

CELIA

Yes, what about him?

CORIN

If you'd like to see a scene played out between a man growing pale with unrequited love and a woman glowing with scorn and proud disdain, come with me a short distance and you'll witness it.

ROSALIND

(speaking so that only CELIA *can hear)* Come on, let's go. The sight of lovers nourishes whoever else is in love. *(to* CORIN*)* Bring us to this little show, and I'll take a part in their play.

They all exit.

ACT 3, SCENE 5

Enter SILVIUS *and* PHOEBE

SILVIUS

Sweet Phoebe, do not scorn me. Do not, Phoebe.
Say that you love me not, but say not so
In bitterness. The common executioner,
Whose heart th' accustomed sight of death makes hard,
5   Falls not the axe upon the humbled neck
But first begs pardon. Will you sterner be
Than he that dies and lives by bloody drops?

Enter ROSALIND, CELIA, *and* CORIN, *behind*

PHOEBE

I would not be thy executioner.
I fly thee, for I would not injure thee.
10   Thou tell'st me there is murder in mine eye.
'Tis pretty, sure, and very probable
That eyes, that are the frail'st and softest things,
Who shut their coward gates on atomies,
Should be called tyrants, butchers, murderers.
15   Now I do frown on thee with all my heart,
And if mine eyes can wound, now let them kill thee.
Now counterfeit to swoon, why, now fall down;
Or if thou canst not, Oh, for shame, for shame,
Lie not, to say mine eyes are murderers.
20   Now show the wound mine eye hath made in thee.
Scratch thee but with a pin, and there remains
Some scar of it. Lean upon a rush,
The cicatrice and capable impressure
Thy palm some moment keeps. But now mine eyes,
25   Which I have darted at thee, hurt thee not.
Nor, I am sure, there is no force in eyes
That can do hurt.

ACT 3, SCENE 5

SILVIUS *and* PHOEBE *enter.*

SILVIUS

> Sweet Phoebe, do not scorn me. Do not, Phoebe. Go ahead and say you don't love me, but not so bitterly. The executioner, who's seen death so much his heart has grown hard, still says, "forgive me" before he drops the axe on the criminal's neck. Are you going to be crueler than the man who makes his living by killing?

ROSALIND, CELIA, *and* CORIN *enter at the back of the stage, unseen.*

PHOEBE

> I don't want to be your executioner: I'm trying to avoid you so that I won't hurt you. You tell me my eyes are murderous—that's a very pretty sentiment, and oh-so-probable, that my frail, soft eyes (which are so cowardly that they close their gates against dust) are tyrants, butchers, and murderers. I'm frowning at you with all my might right now. If my eyes can injure, let them kill you now. Go ahead. Faint, fall down—if you don't, then you're lying about my eyes being murderers. Come on, show me the wound that my eyes have caused. If you get scratched with a pin, it leaves a scar; even if you lean on a rush, it leaves an impression on your palm. But my eyes, which I've darted at you, haven't even left a mark. Now I am sure that eyes can't hurt a person.

SILVIUS
O dear Phoebe,
If ever—as that ever may be near—
You meet in some fresh cheek the power of fancy,
Then shall you know the wounds invisible
That love's keen arrows make.

PHOEBE
But till that time
Come not thou near me. And when that time comes,
Afflict me with thy mocks, pity me not,
As till that time I shall not pity thee.

ROSALIND
(advancing, as Ganymede) And why, I pray you? Who
might be your mother,
That you insult, exult, and all at once,
Over the wretched? What though you have no beauty—
As, by my faith, I see no more in you
Than without candle may go dark to bed—
Must you be therefore proud and pitiless?
Why, what means this? Why do you look on me?
I see no more in you than in the ordinary
Of nature's sale-work.—'Od's my little life,
I think she means to tangle my eyes, too.
—No, faith, proud mistress, hope not after it.
'Tis not your inky brows, your black silk hair,
Your bugle eyeballs, nor your cheek of cream
That can entame my spirits to your worship.
—You foolish shepherd, wherefore do you follow her,
Like foggy south puffing with wind and rain?
You are a thousand times a properer man
Than she a woman. 'Tis such fools as you
That makes the world full of ill-favored children.
'Tis not her glass but you that flatters her,
And out of you she sees herself more proper
Than any of her lineaments can show her.

SILVIUS

Oh, darling Phoebe, if you ever fall in love with some fresh face, then you'll know about the invisible wounds that love's sharp arrows can make.

PHOEBE

Well, until that time, don't come near me. And when that time comes, then you can mock me, but please don't pity me, because I won't pity you.

ROSALIND

(coming forward, speaking as Ganymede) And why, please tell me? Is your mother a goddess that you would insult a wretched man, and exult over the injury you've caused him, all at the same time? You're not beautiful—really, you're not so pretty that you could go to bed with the lights on—so why must you act so proud and pitiless? Wait a minute, what's going on? Why are you looking at me like that? I don't see anything in you but nature's usual handiwork.—Oh, for God's sake, I think she also wants me to fall in love with her. No, proud woman, don't hope for that. Not even your black eyebrows, your silky black hair, your beady black eyeballs, or your yellowish-white complexion can make me worship you. You foolish shepherd: why are you following her, raining tears and puffing hot air like a foggy south wind? You are a thousand times better than she. It's fools like you who, marrying badly, fill the world with ugly children. It's not her mirror but *you* who insists she's beautiful. The image of herself that she gets from you is better than her actual features.

60 —But, mistress, know yourself. Down on your knees
 And thank heaven, fasting, for a good man's love,
 For I must tell you friendly in your ear,
 Sell when you can; you are not for all markets.
 Cry the man mercy, love him, take his offer.
65 Foul is most foul, being foul to be a scoffer.
 —So take her to thee, shepherd. Fare you well.

PHOEBE
 Sweet youth, I pray you chide a year together.
 I had rather hear you chide than this man woo.

ROSALIND
 He's fall'n in love with your foulness. *(to* SILVIUS*)* And
70 she'll fall in love with my anger. If it be so, as fast as she
 answers thee with frowning looks, I'll sauce her with bitter
 words. *(to* PHOEBE*)* Why look you so upon me?

PHOEBE
 For no ill will I bear you.

ROSALIND
 I pray you, do not fall in love with me,
75 For I am falser than vows made in wine.
 Besides, I like you not. If you will know my house,
 'Tis at the tuft of olives, here hard by.
 —Will you go, sister?—Shepherd, ply her hard.
 —Come, sister.—Shepherdess, look on him better,
80 And be not proud. Though all the world could see,
 None could be so abused in sight as he.
 —Come, to our flock.

      Exeunt ROSALIND, CELIA *and* CORIN

PHOEBE
 Dead shepherd, now I find thy saw of might:
 "Who ever loved that loved not at first sight?"

But mistress, know yourself. Get down on your knees and thank heaven for sending you such a good man. I'm telling you, as a friend, that you should sell while the market's good—you're not going to have many more buyers. Ask this man's forgiveness, love him, and accept his offer. You're already ugly, don't make matters worse by being scornful, too. So take her, shepherd, and God bless you.

PHOEBE

Sweet boy, I'd rather hear you scold me for a whole year than this man woo me for a minute.

ROSALIND

He's fallen in love with your sheer ugliness. *(To* SIL-VIUS*)* And I think she's falling in love with my anger. If I'm right, as soon as she answers you with frowns, I'll rebuke her with bitter words. *(to* PHOEBE*)* Why are you looking at me like that?

PHOEBE

I don't wish you any harm.

ROSALIND

I'm telling you, don't fall in love with me. I'm more false than the promises a man makes while drunk. Besides, I don't like you. If you'd like to know where I live, my house is in the olive grove close by. —Come on, sister. —Shepherd, keep working on her. —Come on, sister. —Shepherdess, give him another chance. And don't be proud. The whole world could look at you, and no one would be as blind as he is, thinking you're beautiful. —Come on, to our sheep.

ROSALIND, CELIA, *and* CORIN *exit.*

PHOEBE

The "shepherd" is the writer Christopher Marlowe, a contemporary of Shakespeare's who died in 1593.

Dead shepherd, now I understand what you meant when you said, "You've never loved until you've fallen in love at first sight."

SILVIUS

85   Sweet Phoebe—

PHOEBE

Ha, what sayst thou, Silvius?

SILVIUS

Sweet Phoebe, pity me.

PHOEBE

Why, I am sorry for thee, gentle Silvius.

SILVIUS

Wherever sorrow is, relief would be.

90   If you do sorrow at my grief in love,
By giving love your sorrow and my grief
Were both extermined.

PHOEBE

Thou hast my love. Is not that neighborly?

SILVIUS

I would have you.

PHOEBE

95   Why, that were covetousness.
Silvius, the time was that I hated thee,
And yet it is not that I bear thee love,
But since that thou canst talk of love so well,
Thy company, which erst was irksome to me,

100   I will endure, and I'll employ thee too.
But do not look for further recompense
Than thine own gladness that thou art employed.

SILVIUS

So holy and so perfect is my love,
And I in such a poverty of grace,

105   That I shall think it a most plenteous crop
To glean the broken ears after the man
That the main harvest reaps. Loose now and then
A scattered smile, and that I'll live upon.

PHOEBE

Know'st thou the youth that spoke to me erewhile?

SILVIUS

Sweet Phoebe—

PHOEBE

What? Did you say something, Silvius?

SILVIUS

Sweet Phoebe, have pity on me.

PHOEBE

Well, I'm sorry for you, gentle Silvius.

SILVIUS

But if you're really sorry for me, you can cure me. If you're sorry for the grief I feel in loving you, you can love me back. Then both my grief and your sorrow will be cured.

PHOEBE

You have my friendship. Isn't that enough?

SILVIUS

I want you.

PHOEBE

Well, that's just greedy. Silvius, I used to hate you. I still don't love you, but since you're well-spoken when it comes to love, I'll keep you around and make use of you. But don't expect any more than that.

SILVIUS

My love for you is so pure and perfect, and I'm in such a bad way, that I'll be grateful for whatever leftover love you throw my way. Every once in a while, toss me a distracted smile, and I'll live on that.

PHOEBE

Do you know the boy who was just speaking to me?

SILVIUS

110   Not very well, but I have met him oft,
           And he hath bought the cottage and the bounds
           That the old carlot once was master of.

PHOEBE

           Think not I love him, though I ask for him.
           'Tis but a peevish boy—yet he talks well—
115   But what care I for words? Yet words do well
           When he that speaks them pleases those that hear.
           It is a pretty youth—not very pretty—
           But sure he's proud—and yet his pride becomes him.
           He'll make a proper man. The best thing in him
120   Is his complexion; and faster than his tongue
           Did make offense, his eye did heal it up.
           He is not very tall—yet for his years he's tall.
           His leg is but so-so—and yet 'tis well.
           There was a pretty redness in his lip,
125   A little riper and more lusty red
           Than that mixed in his cheek: 'twas just the difference
           Betwixt the constant red and mingled damask.
           There be some women, Silvius, had they marked him
           In parcels as I did, would have gone near
130   To fall in love with him; but for my part
           I love him not nor hate him not; and yet
           I have more cause to hate him than to love him.
           For what had he to do to chide at me?
           He said mine eyes were black and my hair black
135   And, now I am remembered, scorned at me.
           I marvel why I answered not again.
           But that's all one: omittance is no quittance.
           I'll write to him a very taunting letter,
           And thou shalt bear it. Wilt thou, Silvius?

SILVIUS

140   Phoebe, with all my heart.

SILVIUS

Not very well, but I've met him several times. He's bought the cottage and the grounds that the old peasant used to own.

PHOEBE

Don't think I'm in love with him just because I'm asking about him. He's an irritable boy, though he speaks well. But what do I care about words? And yet, words are a good thing when the man speaking them is pleasant to listen to. He's good-looking, but not too good-looking. He's awfully proud, but his pride suits him. He'll grow up to be a proper man. The best thing about him is his complexion: as fast as he offends me with words, his pretty face heals the wound. He's not very tall, but he's tall enough for his age. His legs aren't great, but they're alright. His lips were nice and red, a little more lively and passionate than the red that was in his cheeks—one was pure red and the other more pink. There are women out there, Silvius, who would have nearly fallen in love with him after inspecting him as closely as I have. But I don't love him or hate him—though I suppose I have more reason to hate him than love him. What right did he have to scold me like that? He said my eyes and my hair were black and, now that I think of it, he scorned me. I'm surprised I didn't bite back. But no matter—I'll get back at him soon enough. I'll write him a taunting letter, and you can deliver it. Will you do that for me, Silvius?

SILVIUS

With all my heart, Phoebe.

PHOEBE
I'll write it straight.
The matter's in my head and in my heart.
I will be bitter with him and passing short.
Go with me, Silvius.

Exeunt

PHOEBE

I'll write it right now—the whole thing is pressing on my mind, and on my heart. I'll be bitter toward him, and curt. Come with me, Silvius.

They exit.

ACT FOUR
SCENE 1

Enter ROSALIND, CELIA, *and* JAQUES

JAQUES

I prithee, pretty youth, let me be better acquainted with
thee.

ROSALIND

They say you are a melancholy fellow.

JAQUES

I am so. I do love it better than laughing.

ROSALIND

5   Those that are in extremity of either are abominable fellows
and betray themselves to every modern censure worse than
drunkards.

JAQUES

Why, 'tis good to be sad and say nothing.

ROSALIND

Why then, 'tis good to be a post.

JAQUES

10   I have neither the scholar's melancholy, which is emulation;
nor the musician's, which is fantastical; nor the courtier's,
which is proud; nor the soldier's, which is ambitious; nor
the lawyer's, which is politic; nor the lady's, which is nice;
nor the lover's, which is all these, but it is a melancholy of
15   mine own, compounded of many simples, extracted from
many objects, and indeed the sundry contemplation of my
travels, in which my often rumination wraps me in a most
humorous sadness.

ACT FOUR

SCENE 1

ROSALIND, CELIA, *and* JAQUES *enter.*

JAQUES

Please, pretty young man, I'd like to get to know you better.

ROSALIND

They say you are a melancholy fellow.

JAQUES

I am. I like it better than laughing.

ROSALIND

People who are either too serious or too silly are awful. They make themselves targets for ridicule even faster than drunks do.

JAQUES

Well, I think it's good to be serious and keep quiet.

ROSALIND

In that case it's good to be a post.

JAQUES

I'm not a scholar's kind of melancholy, which is all about impressing one's peers, or a musician's, which comes from his passion for his art. I don't have the proud melancholy of a courtier or the ambitious melancholy of a soldier or the calculated melancholy of a lawyer. My melancholy is not like a lady's—which is nothing more than an affectation—nor like a lover's, which combines all of these qualities. My melancholy is purely my own—a compound made from many ingredients. I'm serious because I've traveled so much. When I think about all the things I've seen, I sink into deep thoughts.

ROSALIND

20
A traveler. By my faith, you have great reason to be sad. I
fear you have sold your own lands to see other men's. Then
to have seen much and to have nothing is to have rich eyes
and poor hands.

JAQUES

Yes, I have gained my experience.

ROSALIND

And your experience makes you sad. I had rather have a
25
fool to make me merry than experience to make me sad—
and to travel for it, too.

Enter ORLANDO

ORLANDO

Good day and happiness, dear Rosalind.

JAQUES

Nay then, God be wi' you, an you talk in blank verse.

ROSALIND

30
Farewell, Monsieur Traveler. Look you lisp and wear
strange suits, disable all the benefits of your own country,
be out of love with your nativity, and almost chide God for
making you that countenance you are, or I will scarce think
you have swam in a gondola.

Exit JAQUES

35
(as Ganymede pretending to be ROSALIND*)* Why, how now,
Orlando, where have you been all this while? You a lover?
An you serve me such another trick, never come in my sight
more.

ORLANDO

My fair Rosalind, I come within an hour of my promise.

ROSALIND

You're a traveler. Well then, you have good reason to be sad. I'm afraid you've sold your own land to see other men's. To have seen much but own nothing is to have rich eyes and poor hands.

JAQUES

Not true. I gained my experience.

ROSALIND

And your experience makes you sad. I'd rather have a jester to make me happy than experience to make me sad—and to travel for all that trouble, no less!

ORLANDO *enters.*

ORLANDO

Good day and happiness to you, darling Rosalind.

JAQUES

No—I'll say goodbye if you're going to talk in blank verse.

This is a joke: most of the play is in blank (un-rhymed) verse.

ROSALIND

Goodbye, Mr. Traveler. Make sure to keep up your foreign accent, wear strange clothes, belittle all the benefits you receive from your native land and fall out of love with it, and nearly curse God for making you look like the Englishman you are, or else I'll never believe you've paddled in a gondola in a Venetian canal, as you say you have.

JAQUES *exits.*

(as Ganymede pretending to be ROSALIND*)* What's going on, Orlando? Where have you been all this time? And you call yourself a lover? If you ever insult me like this again, don't bother coming around here again.

ORLANDO

My beautiful Rosalind, I'm only an hour late.

ROSALIND

40   Break an hour's promise in love? He that will divide a
      minute into a thousand parts and break but a part of the
      thousand part of a minute in the affairs of love, it may be
      said of him that Cupid hath clapped him o' th' shoulder,
      but I'll warrant him heart-whole.

ORLANDO

45   Pardon me, dear Rosalind.

ROSALIND

      Nay, an you be so tardy, come no more in my sight. I had as
      lief be wooed of a snail.

ORLANDO

      Of a snail?

ROSALIND

      Ay, of a snail, for though he comes slowly, he carries his
50   house on his head—a better jointure, I think, than you
      make a woman. Besides, he brings his destiny with him.

ORLANDO

      What's that?

ROSALIND

      Why, horns, which such as you are fain to be beholding to
      your wives for. But he comes armed in his fortune and
55   prevents the slander of his wife.

ORLANDO

      Virtue is no hornmaker, and my Rosalind is virtuous.

ROSALIND

      And I am your Rosalind.

CELIA

      (as Aliena) It pleases him to call you so, but he hath a
      Rosalind of a better leer than you.

ROSALIND

You'd break a date with your beloved by a whole hour? A man who will dare to meet his lover even a *thousandth* part of a minute late—well, it's possible he likes her, but I doubt he really loves the woman.

ORLANDO

Forgive me, darling Rosalind.

ROSALIND

No, if you're ever late like this again, I'll refuse to see you. I'd rather be wooed by a snail.

ORLANDO

A snail?

ROSALIND

Yes, a snail. Because even though he's slow, he carries his house on his head—a better offer than you can make a woman, I think. Besides, he brings his fate with him.

ORLANDO

What fate is that?

ROSALIND

Why, his cuckold's horns, of course—the kind you men are always blaming on your wives. See, the snail already has its horns, which prevents nasty rumors from spreading about his wife's infidelity.

ORLANDO

A virtuous woman won't give her husband horns, and my Rosalind is definitely virtuous.

ROSALIND

And I am your Rosalind.

CELIA

(as Aliena) He likes calling you that, but he's got another Rosalind out there with a prettier face.

ROSALIND

60   Come, woo me, woo me, for now I am in a holiday humor,
        and like enough to consent. What would you say to me now,
        an I were your very, very Rosalind?

ORLANDO

        I would kiss before I spoke.

ROSALIND

        Nay, you were better speak first, and when you were
65   graveled for lack of matter, you might take occasion to kiss.
        Very good orators, when they are out, they will spit; and for
        lovers lacking—God warn us—matter, the cleanliest shift
        is to kiss.

ORLANDO

        How if the kiss be denied?

ROSALIND

70   Then she puts you to entreaty, and there begins new matter.

ORLANDO

        Who could be out, being before his beloved mistress?

ROSALIND

        Marry, that should you if I were your mistress, or I should
        think my honesty ranker than my wit.

ORLANDO

        What, of my suit?

ROSALIND

75   Not out of your apparel, and yet out of your suit. Am not I
        your Rosalind?

ROSALIND

Come on, woo me, woo me. I'm in a good mood now and likely to give you what you want. What would you say to me now if I really were your precious little Rosalind?

ORLANDO

I'd kiss you before I spoke.

ROSALIND

No, it would be better to speak first and kiss only after you've run out of things to say. When good orators finish talking, they spit; when lovers do (God help us if they ever do), they kiss.

ORLANDO

What if she won't kiss me?

ROSALIND

Then she's making you beg, and that gives you a whole new set of things to talk about.

ORLANDO

Who could be out of things to say if he were with the girl he loves?

ROSALIND

Indeed, you would be out if I were your mistress—if my chastity is worth as much as my wit.

ORLANDO

Would I be out of my suit?

"Out of my suit" here means he'd have to end his courtship of Rosalind (suit is used in the legal sense). Rosalind takes him to mean a suit of clothes.

ROSALIND

No, you'd still have your clothes on—but, yes, I wouldn't think much of you. Aren't I your Rosalind?

ORLANDO

I take some joy to say you are because I would be talking of her.

ROSALIND

Well, in her person I say I will not have you.

ORLANDO

80   Then, in mine own person I die.

ROSALIND

No, faith, die by attorney. The poor world is almost six thousand years old, and in all this time there was not any man died in his own person, videlicet, in a love cause. Troilus had his brains dashed out with a Grecian club, yet

85   he did what he could to die before, and he is one of the patterns of love. Leander, he would have lived many a fair year though Hero had turned nun if it had not been for a hot midsummer night, for, good youth, he went but forth to wash him in the Hellespont and, being taken with the

90   cramp, was drowned; and the foolish chroniclers of that age found it was Hero of Sestos. But these are all lies. Men have died from time to time, and worms have eaten them, but not for love.

ORLANDO

I would not have my right Rosalind of this mind, for I

95   protest her frown might kill me.

ROSALIND

By this hand, it will not kill a fly. But come; now I will be your Rosalind in a more coming-on disposition, and ask me what you will, I will grant it.

ORLANDO

Then love me, Rosalind.

ROSALIND

100   Yes, faith, will I, Fridays and Saturdays and all.

ORLANDO

And wilt thou have me?

ORLANDO

I like to pretend you are, because then it's almost like actually talking to her.

ROSALIND

Well, on behalf of Rosalind, I'll tell you I don't want you.

ORLANDO

Then, on behalf of myself, I'll tell you I'll die.

ROSALIND

No, you won't die yourself, but only by proxy. This world is almost six thousand years old, and in all this time not one man has ever actually died from love. Troilus may have wanted to die from love, and he's now considered one of the great, tragic love heroes, but, in fact, a Greek with a club beat his brains out. It had nothing to do with love. Leander would have lived many more years if it hadn't been for a particularly hot summer night, when he went swimming in the Hellespont, got a cramp, and drowned. The foolish poets of the time insisted he died for love, but they're lying. All the love stories are lies. Men have died from time to time, and worms have eaten them, but not because of love.

> According to ancient myth, Troilus, Cressida's lover, was killed by the warrior Achilles. Leander drowned while swimming across the Hellespont to visit his lover, Hero. Both were described and redescribed through the ages as tragic lovers.

ORLANDO

I hope Rosalind doesn't feel as you do. Her frown alone would kill me.

ROSALIND

No, her frown wouldn't kill a fly. But come on, now I'll play your Rosalind, and in a more friendly state of mind. Whatever you ask for, I'll give.

ORLANDO

Then love me, Rosalind.

ROSALIND

Okay, I will—on Fridays and Saturdays, and the rest.

ORLANDO

And will you have me?

ROSALIND
Ay, and twenty such.

ORLANDO
What sayest thou?

ROSALIND
Are you not good?

ORLANDO
105   I hope so.

ROSALIND
Why then, can one desire too much of a good thing?—
Come, sister, you shall be the priest and marry us.—Give
me your hand, Orlando.—What do you say, sister?

ORLANDO
Pray thee, marry us.

CELIA
110   I cannot say the words.

ROSALIND
You must begin "Will you, Orlando—"

CELIA
Go to.—Will you, Orlando, have to wife this Rosalind?

ORLANDO
I will.

ROSALIND
Ay, but when?

ORLANDO
115   Why, now, as fast as she can marry us.

ROSALIND
Then you must say "I take thee, Rosalind, for wife."

ORLANDO
I take thee, Rosalind, for wife.

ROSALIND

Sure, and twenty others just like you.

ORLANDO

What's that?

ROSALIND

Well, aren't you a good man?

ORLANDO

I hope so.

ROSALIND

And can a person ever have too much of a good thing?—Come on, sister, you can be the priest and marry us.—Give me your hand, Orlando.—What do you say, sister?

ORLANDO

Please, marry us.

CELIA

I can't say the words.

As Celia is not a priest, she can't actually perform the ceremony.

ROSALIND

You just have to say, "Do you, Orlando—"

CELIA

Oh, stop it.—Do you, Orlando, take Rosalind to be your lawfully wedded wife?

ORLANDO

I do.

ROSALIND

Okay, but when?

ORLANDO

Right now; as fast as she can say the vows.

ROSALIND

Then you have to say, "I take you, Rosalind, to be my lawfully wedded wife."

ORLANDO

I take you, Rosalind, to be my lawfully wedded wife.

ROSALIND
    I might ask you for your commission, but I do take thee,
    Orlando, for my husband. There's a girl goes before the
120   priest, and certainly a woman's thought runs before her
    actions.

ORLANDO
    So do all thoughts. They are winged.

ROSALIND
    Now tell me how long you would have her after you have
    possessed her.

ORLANDO
125   Forever and a day.

ROSALIND
    Say "a day" without the "ever." No, no, Orlando, men are
    April when they woo, December when they wed. Maids are
    May when they are maids, but the sky changes when they
    are wives. I will be more jealous of thee than a Barbary cock-
130   pigeon over his hen, more clamorous than a parrot against
    rain, more newfangled than an ape, more giddy in my
    desires than a monkey. I will weep for nothing, like Diana
    in the fountain, and I will do that when you are disposed to
    be merry. I will laugh like a hyena, and that when thou art
135   inclined to sleep.

ORLANDO
    But will my Rosalind do so?

ROSALIND
    By my life, she will do as I do.

ORLANDO
    Oh, but she is wise.

ROSALIND

Maybe I should ask you what right you have to take me, but I'll take you, Orlando, to be my husband. Look, I've sped ahead of the priest and answered the question before he even asked. A woman's thoughts are always running ahead of her actions.

ORLANDO

So do all thoughts. They have wings.

ROSALIND

Now tell me how long you intend to keep her.

ORLANDO

Forever and a day.

ROSALIND

You might as well just say for "a day," and forget the "ever" part. No, Orlando, men are like April when they're wooing a girl—young, and passionate—but like December once they're married and their passions have cooled. Women are as sweet and temperate as springtime when they're single, but the climate changes once they're married. I'll be more jealous of you than a wild rooster over his hen; more noisy than a parrot chattering about the rain; more fond of new things than an ape; more giddy about getting what I want than a monkey. I'll cry at nothing, and I'll always do it when you're in a good mood. And when you want to go to sleep, I'll be up laughing like a hyena.

ORLANDO

But will my Rosalind do this, too?

ROSALIND

Indeed, she'll act just like me.

ORLANDO

But she is wise.

ROSALIND

140 Or else she could not have the wit to do this. The wiser, the waywarder. Make the doors upon a woman's wit, and it will out at the casement. Shut that, and 'twill out at the keyhole. Stop that, 'twill fly with the smoke out at the chimney.

ORLANDO

A man that had a wife with such a wit, he might say "Wit, whither wilt?"

ROSALIND

145 Nay, you might keep that check for it, till you met your wife's wit going to your neighbor's bed.

ORLANDO

And what wit could wit have to excuse that?

ROSALIND

Marry, to say she came to seek you there. You shall never take her without her answer unless you take her without her 150 tongue. Oh, that woman that cannot make her fault her husband's occasion, let her never nurse her child herself, for she will breed it like a fool.

ORLANDO

For these two hours, Rosalind, I will leave thee.

ROSALIND

Alas, dear love, I cannot lack thee two hours.

ORLANDO

155 I must attend the duke at dinner. By two o'clock I will be with thee again.

ROSALIND

Ay, go your ways, go your ways. I knew what you would prove. My friends told me as much, and I thought no less. That flattering tongue of yours won me. 'Tis but one cast 160 away, and so, come, death. Two o'clock is your hour?

ROSALIND

Right. If she weren't wise, she wouldn't be smart enough to behave badly. The wiser the woman, the wilder. If you close the doors on a woman's wit, it'll fly out the window. If you shut the windows, it will pour out the keyhole. If you stop up the keyhole, it will escape from the chimney along with the smoke.

ORLANDO

A man with a wife like that might ask, "Hey, wandering wit, where are you off to?"

ROSALIND

Nah, better save the questions for when you find her in your neighbor's bed.

ORLANDO

And what wit could excuse *that*?

ROSALIND

She'll say she was at the neighbor's looking for you. You'll never find her without an answer unless you find her without a tongue. A woman who doesn't know how to make her own indiscretions look like her husband's fault is hardly a woman. And she's hardly fit to be a mother—her child will turn out to be a fool.

ORLANDO

Rosalind, I have to leave you for two hours.

ROSALIND

Oh, no! Darling, I can't live without you for two hours.

ORLANDO

I must join the duke for lunch. I'll be back here with you by two o'clock.

ROSALIND

Oh, go, leave me. I knew you'd turn out this way. My friends told me as much, and I knew it, too. But I was won over by your flattering words. I'm just another girl whom you've cast aside. So, take me, death! You'll be back at two o'clock?

ORLANDO

Ay, sweet Rosalind.

ROSALIND

By my troth, and in good earnest, and so God mend me, and
by all pretty oaths that are not dangerous, if you break one
jot of your promise or come one minute behind your hour,
165   I will think you the most pathetical break-promise and the
most hollow lover and the most unworthy of her you call
Rosalind that may be chosen out of the gross band of the
unfaithful. Therefore beware my censure, and keep your
promise.

ORLANDO

170   With no less religion than if thou wert indeed my Rosalind.
So, adieu.

ROSALIND

Well, time is the old justice that examines all such
offenders, and let time try. Adieu.

Exit ORLANDO

CELIA

You have simply misused our sex in your love-prate. We
175   must have your doublet and hose plucked over your head
and show the world what the bird hath done to her own
nest.

ROSALIND

O coz, coz, coz, my pretty little coz, that thou didst know
how many fathom deep I am in love. But it cannot be
180   sounded; my affection hath an unknown bottom, like the
Bay of Portugal.

CELIA

Or rather bottomless, that as fast as you pour affection in,
it runs out.

ORLANDO

Yes, sweet Rosalind.

ROSALIND

Honestly, truly, in God's name, and by all those little girly oaths that don't actually have any power, if you break even a little bit of your promise, or if you come even a minute after two o'clock, I'll think you the most pathetic promise breaker, the most lying lover, and the most unworthy partner for Rosalind that could be found anywhere. So beware of my contempt, and keep your promise.

ORLANDO

I'll keep my promise just as if you really were Rosalind. So, goodbye.

ROSALIND

Well, time is the old judge that tries your kind of criminal. Time will tell what kind of a man you are. Goodbye.

ORLANDO *exits.*

CELIA

You have absolutely abused our sex in this love talk of yours. We should rip off your man's clothing and show the world the woman who has represented her own kind so badly.

ROSALIND

Oh cousin, cousin, cousin, my sweet little cousin, I wish you knew how deep in love I am. The bottom of my love is so deep it can't be reached. It's as deep as the bay of Portugal.

CELIA

Or it's bottomless, at least: pour affection in one end, and it runs out the other.

ROSALIND
No, that same wicked bastard of Venus that was begot of
185   thought, conceived of spleen, and born of madness, that
blind rascally boy that abuses everyone's eyes because his
own are out, let him be judge how deep I am in love. I'll tell
thee, Aliena, I cannot be out of the sight of Orlando. I'll go
find a shadow and sigh till he come.

CELIA
190   And I'll sleep.

Exeunt

ROSALIND

Cupid—that blind bastard son of Venus, conceived from a thought and anger, born from insanity, that blind, naughty boy who makes everyone else go blind just because he can't see himself—let Cupid judge how deep my love runs. I'm telling you, Aliena, I can't stand being apart from Orlando. I'm going to find some shade and sigh until he returns.

CELIA

And I'm going to sleep.

They exit.

ACT 4, SCENE 2

Enter JAQUES *and* LORDS, *like foresters*

JAQUES
Which is he that killed the deer?

FIRST LORD
Sir, it was I.

JAQUES
Let's present him to the duke like a Roman conqueror. And
it would do well to set the deer's horns upon his head for a
5 branch of victory.—Have you no song, forester, for this
purpose?

SECOND LORD
Yes, sir.

JAQUES
Sing it. 'Tis no matter how it be in tune, so it make noise
enough.

SECOND LORD
(sings)
10 *What shall he have that killed the deer?*
His leather skin and horns to wear.
Then sing him home.
(The rest shall bear this burden.)
Take thou no scorn to wear the horn.
15 *It was a crest ere thou wast born.*
Thy father's father wore it,
And thy father bore it.
The horn, the horn, the lusty horn
Is not a thing to laugh to scorn.

Exeunt

ACT 4, SCENE 2

JAQUES *enters with* LORDS, *dressed like foresters.*

JAQUES

Which one of you killed the deer?

FIRST LORD

It was me, sir.

JAQUES

Let's bring this man to the duke, like a triumphant Roman conqueror. Put the deer's horns on his head, like a victory branch. Do you have a song, forester, for this occasion?

SECOND LORD

Yes, sir.

JAQUES

Then sing it. It doesn't matter if it's in tune so long as it's loud enough.

SECOND LORD

(sings)
What should we give to the man who killed this deer?
Give him the hide and the horns to wear.
Then sing this song to send him home
(The other LORDS *pick up the deer)*
Don't be ashamed to wear the horns.
They've been worn since before you were born.
Your father's father wore it,
And your father endured it.
The horn, the horn, the lustful horn
Is not to be laughed at or scorned.

They all exit.

ACT 4, SCENE 3

Enter ROSALIND *and* CELIA

ROSALIND

How say you now? Is it not past two o'clock? And here
much Orlando.

CELIA

I warrant you, with pure love and troubled brain he hath
ta'en his bow and arrows and is gone forth to sleep.

Enter SILVIUS

5   Look who comes here.

SILVIUS

(to ROSALIND*)* My errand is to you, fair youth.
My gentle Phoebe did bid me give you this.
I know not the contents, but as I guess
By the stern brow and waspish action
10   Which she did use as she was writing of it,
It bears an angry tenor. Pardon me.
I am but as a guiltless messenger.
(Gives the letter)

ROSALIND

(Examines the letter) (as Ganymede)
Patience herself would startle at this letter
And play the swaggerer. Bear this, bear all.
15   She says I am not fair, that I lack manners.
She calls me proud, and that she could not love me
Were man as rare as phoenix. 'Od's my will,
Her love is not the hare that I do hunt.
Why writes she so to me? Well, shepherd, well,
20   This is a letter of your own device.

SILVIUS

No, I protest, I know not the contents.
Phoebe did write it.

ACT 4, SCENE 3

ROSALIND *and* CELIA *enter.*

ROSALIND

What do you say now? Isn't it past two o'clock? And I see a lot of Orlando here.

CELIA

I'm telling you, he's taken his bow and arrows and, with a pure love and a worried brain, has gone to take a nap. Look who's coming.

SILVIUS *enters.*

SILVIUS

(to ROSALIND*)* I've been sent to find you, young man. My lovely Phoebe told me to give you this letter. I don't know what's in it, but guessing from her stern expression and her wasp-like demeanor as she was writing it, I bet she's angry. You'll have to excuse me, as I'm just the messenger.

ROSALIND

(reading the letter as Ganymede) Patience herself would be shocked by this letter and become feisty. If I can take this, I can take anything. She says I'm not handsome and have no manners. She says I'm arrogant and that she couldn't love me even if men were as rare as the mythical phoenix. Honestly! I'm not hunting after her love. Why would she write this way to me? Tell the truth, shepherd: you wrote this letter.

SILVIUS

No, I swear, I don't even know what's in it. Phoebe wrote it.

ROSALIND
  Come, come, you are a fool,
  And turned into the extremity of love.
25 I saw her hand. She has a leathern hand,
  A freestone-colored hand. I verily did think
  That her old gloves were on, but 'twas her hands.
  She has a huswife's hand—but that's no matter.
  I say she never did invent this letter.
30 This is a man's invention, and his hand.

SILVIUS
  Sure it is hers.

ROSALIND
  Why, 'tis a boisterous and a cruel style,
  A style for challengers. Why, she defies me
  Like Turk to Christian. Women's gentle brain
35 Could not drop forth such giant-rude invention,
  Such Ethiop words, blacker in their effect
  Than in their countenance. Will you hear the letter?

SILVIUS
  So please you, for I never heard it yet,
  Yet heard too much of Phoebe's cruelty.

ROSALIND
40 She Phoebes me. Mark how the tyrant writes.
  (reads) Art thou god to shepherd turned,
  That a maiden's heart hath burned?
  Can a woman rail thus?

SILVIUS
  Call you this railing?

ROSALIND
  (reads)
45 Why, thy godhead laid apart,
  Warr'st thou with a woman's heart?
  Did you ever hear such railing?
  Whiles the eye of man did woo me,
  That could do no vengeance to me.
50 Meaning me a beast.

ROSALIND

Come on, you're a fool, and driven to extreme measures by love. I saw her hands: they were as rough as leather and just as brown; I thought she was wearing old gloves, but they were, in fact, her hands. These are the hands of a hard-working housewife, but that's not the point. The point is that she didn't write this letter. These are a man's words, and his handwriting.

SILVIUS

I'm telling you, it's hers.

ROSALIND

Well, it's written in a boisterous and rude style—someone is up for a fight. Why, she challenges me like a Muslim would challenge a Christian. No, a woman's gentle brain could never have come up with such crude expressions and even harsher meanings. Do you want to hear what she says?

SILVIUS

If you want to read it, as I haven't heard it yet, though I've heard too much of Phoebe's cruelty.

ROSALIND

She's Phoebe-ing me. Listen to what the tyrant says. *(reading)* "Are you a god disguised as a shepherd, that you know so expertly how to burn my heart?" Now, honestly, would a woman rant like this?

SILVIUS

You call that ranting?

ROSALIND

(reading) "Why have you set aside your divine nature just to battle with a woman's affections?" Did you ever hear such ranting? *(reading)* "When other men have wooed me, they didn't hurt me." In other words, she thinks I'm not a man, but an animal.

If the scorn of your bright eyne
Have power to raise such love in mine,
Alack, in me what strange effect
Would they work in mild aspect?
55   Whiles you chid me, I did love.
How then might your prayers move?
He that brings this love to thee
Little knows this love in me,
And by him seal up thy mind
60   Whether that thy youth and kind
Will the faithful offer take
Of me, and all that I can make,
Or else by him my love deny,
And then I'll study how to die.

SILVIUS
65   Call you this chiding?

CELIA
(as Aliena) Alas, poor shepherd.

ROSALIND
Do you pity him? No, he deserves no pity.—Wilt thou love
such a woman? What, to make thee an instrument and play
false strains upon thee? Not to be endured. Well, go your
70   way to her, for I see love hath made thee a tame snake, and
say this to her: that if she love me, I charge her to love thee;
if she will not, I will never have her unless thou entreat for
her. If you be a true lover, hence and not a word, for here
comes more company.

Exit SILVIUS

Enter OLIVER

OLIVER
75   Good morrow, fair ones. Pray you, if you know,
Where in the purlieus of this forest stands
A sheepcote fenced about with olive trees?

(reading) "If the scorn in your bright eyes can make me fall so deeply in love, can you imagine what power they might have if they looked at me more kindly? While you sneered at me, I loved you. Consider what effect kind prayers might have. The man that brings you this letter doesn't know how I feel about you. Send me your answer via him. Tell me via him whether you will accept my faithful offer of myself and all that I can do. Or tell him you will deny my love, in which case I'll figure out how to die."

SILVIUS

You call this sneering?

CELIA

(as Aliena) Oh, you poor shepherd!

ROSALIND

Why do you pity him? He doesn't deserve any pity. (*to* SILVIUS) Why would you love such a woman? So she can turn you into an instrument and play lousy tunes on you? It's unbearable. Well, go back to her—I can tell she's turned you into a perfectly tame snake—and tell her this: if she loves me, I command her to love you. And if she won't love you, tell her I'll never take her unless you beg me to. If you're a true lover, get out of here. No, don't say another word, because here comes more company.

SILVIUS *exits.*

OLIVER enters.

OLIVER

Good morning, pretty ones. Tell me, if you know: where in this forest is there a shepherd's cottage surrounded by olive trees?

CELIA

(as Aliena)
West of this place, down in the neighbor bottom,
The rank of osiers by the murmuring stream

80   Left on your right hand brings you to the place.
But at this hour the house doth keep itself.
There's none within.

OLIVER

If that an eye may profit by a tongue,
Then should I know you by description.

85   Such garments, and such years. "The boy is fair,
Of female favor, and bestows himself
Like a ripe sister; the woman low
And browner than her brother." Are not you
The owner of the house I did inquire for?

CELIA

90   It is no boast, being asked, to say we are.

OLIVER

Orlando doth commend him to you both,
And to that youth he calls his Rosalind
He sends this bloody napkin. Are you he?

ROSALIND

(as Ganymede) I am. What must we understand by this?

OLIVER

95   Some of my shame, if you will know of me
What man I am, and how, and why, and where
This handkercher was stained.

CELIA

I pray you, tell it.

CELIA

West of here, in the valley next to us. Passing by on your right, there is a row of willows. Follow them straight to the cottage. But right now, the house is keeping to itself— there's no one home.

OLIVER

I think I recognize you from a description I was given of your clothing and age: "The boy is pretty and feminine, and carries himself like a blooming young woman. The woman is short, with a darker complexion than her brother." Aren't you the owners of the house I was just asking about?

CELIA

Since you asked, I suppose it's not bragging to say that we are.

OLIVER

Orlando sends his regards to you both, and he sends this bloody handkerchief to the boy he calls "his Rosalind." Is that you?

ROSALIND

It is. What does this mean?

OLIVER

It's a story that involves some shame on my part. It's about who I am, and how, why, and where this handkerchief was stained.

CELIA

Please, tell us.

OLIVER
When last the young Orlando parted from you,
100   He left a promise to return again
Within an hour, and pacing through the forest,
Chewing the food of sweet and bitter fancy,
Lo, what befell. He threw his eye aside—
And mark what object did present itself:
105   Under an old oak, whose boughs were mossed with age
And high top bald with dry antiquity,
A wretched, ragged man, o'ergrown with hair,
Lay sleeping on his back. About his neck
A green and gilded snake had wreathed itself,
110   Who with her head, nimble in threats, approached
The opening of his mouth. But suddenly,
Seeing Orlando, it unlinked itself
And, with indented glides, did slip away
Into a bush, under which bush's shade
115   A lioness, with udders all drawn dry,
Lay couching, head on ground, with catlike watch
When that the sleeping man should stir—for 'tis
The royal disposition of that beast
To prey on nothing that doth seem as dead.
120   This seen, Orlando did approach the man
And found it was his brother, his elder brother.

CELIA
Oh, I have heard him speak of that same brother,
And he did render him the most unnatural
That lived amongst men.

OLIVER
125   And well he might so do,
For well I know he was unnatural.

ROSALIND
But to Orlando: did he leave him there,
Food to the sucked and hungry lioness?

OLIVER

When young Orlando left you last, he promised to return within an hour. He was pacing through the forest, thinking bittersweet thoughts of love, and listen what happened! He looked to the side, and pay attention to what he saw then: under an oak tree—whose lower branches were mossy with age and top branches ancient and brittle—he saw a wretched beggar, with overgrown hair and beard, asleep on his back. A green and gold snake had wound itself around this man's neck and was slowly making its way toward the man's mouth. However, when it saw Orlando, it unwound itself and slunk away into a bush. But there happened to be a lioness crouching under that bush. Her cubs had nursed from her until she was dry, so she was ravenously hungry, and she was lying with her head on the ground, watching the man as cats do and waiting to see if he would wake up—a lion won't prey on anything that seems dead. Seeing the lioness, Orlando approached the sleeping man. He discovered that the man was his older brother.

CELIA

Oh, I've heard him talk about that brother, and he described him as the most inhumane man alive.

OLIVER

And he was right. I know exactly how inhumane he was.

ROSALIND

But, back to Orlando, did he leave his brother there, to be food for the hungry mother-lioness?

OLIVER
130 Twice did he turn his back and purposed so,
But kindness, nobler ever than revenge,
And nature, stronger than his just occasion,
Made him give battle to the lioness,
Who quickly fell before him; in which hurtling,
From miserable slumber I awaked.

CELIA
135 Are you his brother?

ROSALIND
Was 't you he rescued?

CELIA
Was 't you that did so oft contrive to kill him?

OLIVER
'Twas I, but 'tis not I. I do not shame
To tell you what I was, since my conversion
140 So sweetly tastes, being the thing I am.

ROSALIND
But for the bloody napkin?

OLIVER
By and by.
When from the first to last betwixt us two
Tears our recountments had most kindly bathed—
145 As how I came into that desert place—
In brief, he led me to the gentle duke,
Who gave me fresh array and entertainment,
Committing me unto my brother's love,
Who led me instantly unto his cave,
150 There stripped himself, and here upon his arm
The lioness had torn some flesh away,
Which all this while had bled. And now he fainted,
And cried in fainting upon Rosalind.
Brief, I recovered him, bound up his wound,
155 And after some small space, being strong at heart,

OLIVER

He turned away twice and almost left him there. But his kindness was nobler than even his desire for revenge, his natural goodness was stronger than his need to give his brother what he deserved. He fought the lioness and quickly defeated her. I woke from my miserable sleep when I heard the noise of their struggle.

CELIA

Are you his brother?

ROSALIND

Was it you that he rescued?

CELIA

Was it you that was always plotting to kill him?

OLIVER

That was me, but it's not me— I'm not ashamed to tell you what I once was, since I'm so happy to have since converted.

ROSALIND

But what about the bloody handkerchief?

OLIVER

I'll get there. When we had told each other our entire stories and cried, and I'd told him how I'd ended up in in the forest—well, he brought me to the duke, who gave me fresh clothing and hospitality, and put me in my brother's care. My brother immediately took me to his cave, where he took off his clothing and there on his arm was a wound where the lioness had attacked him, ripping off some of his flesh. The wound had been bleeding the entire time. So, now he fainted, and as he fainted, he called out, "Rosalind!" Quickly, I resuscitated him and bound up his wound. After a brief time—as he is a strong, brave man—

He sent me hither, stranger as I am,
To tell this story, that you might excuse
His broken promise, and to give this napkin
Dyed in his blood unto the shepherd youth
160 That he in sport doth call his Rosalind.

ROSALIND *swoons*

CELIA
Why, how now, Ganymede, sweet Ganymede?

OLIVER
Many will swoon when they do look on blood.

CELIA
There is more in it.—Cousin Ganymede.

OLIVER
Look, he recovers.

ROSALIND
165 I would I were at home.

CELIA
We'll lead you thither.
—I pray you, will you take him by the arm?

OLIVER
Be of good cheer, youth. You a man? You lack a man's heart.

ROSALIND
I do so, I confess it. Ah, sirrah, a body would think this was
170 well-counterfeited. I pray you tell your brother how well I
counterfeited. Heigh-ho.

OLIVER
This was not counterfeit. There is too great testimony in
your complexion that it was a passion of earnest.

ROSALIND
Counterfeit, I assure you.

OLIVER
175 Well then, take a good heart and counterfeit to be a man.

he sent me out to find you, even though I'm a stranger to you. He wanted me to tell you this story and beg your forgiveness for his having broken his promise. He wanted me to give this handkerchief, soaked in his blood, to the boy that he jokingly calls his Rosalind.

ROSALIND *faints.*

CELIA

Oh no! Ganymede! Ganymede, sweetheart?

OLIVER

Many people faint when they see blood.

CELIA

There's more to it than that.—Ganymede!

OLIVER

Look, he's recovering.

ROSALIND

I want to go home.

CELIA

We'll take you there. Please, will you take his arm?

OLIVER

Buck up, boy! You're a man? You don't have a man's courage.

ROSALIND

It's true, I confess. Oh, sir, someone would think I was a good fake. Please tell your brother what a convincing show I put on. Whoo-hoo!

OLIVER

That was no show. Your cheeks are too flushed for me to believe that was a fake faint.

ROSALIND

Fake, I'm telling you.

OLIVER

Well, then, be brave and pretend to be a man.

ROSALIND
So I do. But i' faith, I should have been a woman by right.

CELIA
Come, you look paler and paler. Pray you, draw
homewards.—Good sir, go with us.

OLIVER
That will I, for I must bear answer back
180   How you excuse my brother, Rosalind.

ROSALIND
I shall devise something. But I pray you commend my
counterfeiting to him. Will you go?

Exeunt

ROSALIND

That's what I'm doing. But honestly, I should have been a woman.

CELIA

Come on, you keep getting paler. Please, let's go home. Sir, please come with us.

OLIVER

I'll do that, because I have to tell my brother how you forgave him, Rosalind.

ROSALIND

I'll think of something. But please, tell him how well I faked a faint. Will you come with us?

They all exit.

ACT FIVE
SCENE 1

Enter TOUCHSTONE *and* AUDREY

TOUCHSTONE
We shall find a time, Audrey. Patience, gentle Audrey.

AUDREY
Faith, the priest was good enough, for all the old
gentleman's saying.

TOUCHSTONE
A most wicked Sir Oliver, Audrey, a most vile Martext.
5 But, Audrey, there is a youth here in the forest lays claim to
you.

AUDREY
Ay, I know who 'tis. He hath no interest in me in the world.

Enter WILLIAM

Here comes the man you mean.

TOUCHSTONE
It is meat and drink to me to see a clown. By my troth, we
10 that have good wits have much to answer for. We shall be
flouting. We cannot hold.

WILLIAM
Good ev'n, Audrey.

AUDREY
God gi' good ev'n, William.

WILLIAM
And good ev'n to you, sir.

TOUCHSTONE
15 Good ev'n, gentle friend. Cover thy head, cover thy head.
Nay, prithee, be covered. How old are you, friend?

ACT FIVE
SCENE 1

TOUCHSTONE *and* AUDREY *enter.*

TOUCHSTONE

We'll get married at some point, Audrey. Be patient.

AUDREY

Really, the priest was good enough, no matter what that old guy said.

TOUCHSTONE

No, he was wicked and vile. But Audrey, there's a boy in the forest who claims you're his girl.

AUDREY

Yes, I know who you're talking about, but he has no claim on me.

WILLIAM *enters.*

Here comes the man himself.

TOUCHSTONE

It warms my heart to encounter such a country bumpkin. Truly, we witty men can't hold our tongues. We have to mess with the likes of him, we just can't help it.

WILLIAM

Good evening, Audrey.

AUDREY

Good evening, William.

WILLIAM

And good evening to you, sir.

TOUCHSTONE

Good evening to you, good friend. No, no, put your hat back on, put it back on. No, please, keep your head covered. How old are you, friend?

WILLIAM
Five-and-twenty, sir.

TOUCHSTONE
A ripe age. Is thy name William?

WILLIAM
William, sir.

TOUCHSTONE
20   A fair name. Wast born i' th' forest here?

WILLIAM
Ay, sir, I thank God.

TOUCHSTONE
"Thank God." A good answer. Art rich?

WILLIAM
'Faith, sir, so-so.

TOUCHSTONE
"So-so" is good, very good, very excellent good. And yet it
25   is not: it is but so-so. Art thou wise?

WILLIAM
Ay, sir, I have a pretty wit.

TOUCHSTONE
Why, thou sayst well. I do now remember a saying: "The
fool doth think he is wise, but the wise man knows himself
to be a fool." The heathen philosopher, when he had a
30   desire to eat a grape, would open his lips when he put it into
his mouth, meaning thereby that grapes were made to eat
and lips to open. You do love this maid?

WILLIAM
I do, sir.

TOUCHSTONE
Give me your hand. Art thou learned?

WILLIAM
35   No, sir.

WILLIAM

Twenty-five, sir.

TOUCHSTONE

A mature age. Is your name William?

WILLIAM

Yes, it's William, sir.

TOUCHSTONE

A good name. Were you born here in the forest?

WILLIAM

Yes sir, thank God.

TOUCHSTONE

"Thank God"—that's a good answer. Are you rich?

WILLIAM

Well, so-so.

TOUCHSTONE

"So-so" is good, very good, an excellent answer. And then again, it's not so good, but only so-so. Are you wise?

WILLIAM

Yes sir, I'm fairly witty.

TOUCHSTONE

Well, that's a fine answer. I seem to remember a saying: "Only a fool thinks he's wise; the wise man knows that he is, in fact, a fool." When one self-described philosopher wanted to eat grapes, he opened his lips when they entered his mouth, thereby making the theoretical point that grapes were made to be eaten, and lips to open. Do you love this girl?

This line may be in response to William's open-mouthed gape, but it's also cruelly taunting the bumpkin for his narrow experience and how his "philosophy" derives only from that experience.

WILLIAM

I do, sir.

TOUCHSTONE

Give me your hand. Are you educated?

WILLIAM

No, sir.

TOUCHSTONE
  Then learn this of me: to have is to have. For it is a figure in
  rhetoric that drink, being poured out of a cup into a glass,
  by filling the one doth empty the other. For all your writers
  do consent that ipse is "he." Now, you are not ipse, for I am
40 he.

WILLIAM
  Which he, sir?

TOUCHSTONE
  He, sir, that must marry this woman. Therefore, you
  clown, abandon—which is, in the vulgar, "leave"—the
  society—which in the boorish is "company"—of this
45 female—which in the common is "woman"; which
  together is, abandon the society of this female, or, clown,
  thou perishest; or, to thy better understanding, diest; or, to
  wit, I kill thee, make thee away, translate thy life into death,
  thy liberty into bondage. I will deal in poison with thee, or
50 in bastinado, or in steel. I will bandy with thee in faction. I
  will o'errun thee with policy. I will kill thee a hundred and
  fifty ways. Therefore tremble and depart.

AUDREY
  Do, good William.

WILLIAM
  God rest you merry, sir.

                                                         Exit

  Enter CORIN

CORIN
55 Our master and mistress seeks you. Come away, away.

TOUCHSTONE
  Trip, Audrey, trip, Audrey.—I attend, I attend.

                                                       Exeunt

TOUCHSTONE

Then learn this from me: if you have something, you have it. Everyone knows that when you pour a drink out of a cup and into a glass, the cup becomes empty. And all the authorities know that *ipse* is Latin for "he." You are no longer *ipse*, because I am he.

WILLIAM

Which he, sir?

TOUCHSTONE

Why, the he that will marry this woman. Therefore, idiot, abandon (or, in common language, "leave") the society (which in the boorish tongue is "company") of this female—maybe you'll get it if I say "woman," instead. Say it all at once, now: abandon the society of this female, or, simpleton, you'll perish. Let me put it in a way you'll understand: you'll die. Or, rather, I'll kill you, or I'll do away with you, or I'll turn your life into death and your freedom into captivity. I'll poison you, or beat you with a club, or stab you with a sword. I'll bandy you about and overwhelm you with my cleverness. I will, in other words, kill you in three hundred and fifty ways. Therefore, tremble with fear and leave.

AUDREY

Do what he says, William.

WILLIAM

Farewell, sir.

He exits.

CORIN *enters.*

CORIN

Our master and mistress are looking for you. Let's go.

TOUCHSTONE

Hurry up, Audrey, hurry.—I'm coming, I'm coming.

They all exit.

ACT 5, SCENE 2

Enter ORLANDO *and* OLIVER

ORLANDO
    Is 't possible that on so little acquaintance you should like
    her? That, but seeing, you should love her? And loving,
    woo? And wooing, she should grant? And will you persever
    to enjoy her?

OLIVER
5   Neither call the giddiness of it in question, the poverty of
    her, the small acquaintance, my sudden wooing, nor her
    sudden consenting, but say with me "I love Aliena"; say
    with her that she loves me; consent with both that we may
    enjoy each other. It shall be to your good, for my father's
10   house and all the revenue that was old Sir Rowland's will I
    estate upon you, and here live and die a shepherd.

ORLANDO
    You have my consent. Let your wedding be tomorrow.
    Thither will I invite the duke and all's contented followers.
    Go you and prepare Aliena, for look you, here comes my
15   Rosalind.

Enter ROSALIND

ROSALIND
    (as Ganymede) God save you, brother.

OLIVER
    And you, fair sister.

Exit

ROSALIND
    O my dear Orlando, how it grieves me to see thee wear thy
    heart in a scarf.

ACT 5, SCENE 2

ORLANDO *and* OLIVER *enter.*

ORLANDO

Is it really possible that you could like her right after meeting her? And fall in love with her after merely seeing her? And as soon as you fall in love, with her, woo her? And as soon as you woo her, have her accept? And do you really mean to marry her?

OLIVER

Don't question the foolish haste of it all—or her poverty or our short time together or the abruptness of my courtship or the abruptness of her consent—but say with me, "I love Aliena." And say with me that she loves me. Agree to this match, so we can enjoy each other. It will be to your advantage, because I'll leave our father's house and all his property to you, while I live and die a shepherd here in the forest.

ORLANDO

You have my consent. You can be married tomorrow if you want. I'll invite the duke and all of his followers. Go get Aliena ready—because, look, here comes my Rosalind.

ROSALIND *enters.*

ROSALIND

Hello, brother.

OLIVER

And hello to you, fair sister.

He exits.

ROSALIND

Oh, darling Orlando, it's so hard to see you wearing your heart in a sling.

ORLANDO

20   It is my arm.

ROSALIND

I thought thy heart had been wounded with the claws of a
lion.

ORLANDO

Wounded it is, but with the eyes of a lady.

ROSALIND

Did your brother tell you how I counterfeited to swoon
25   when he showed me your handkercher?

ORLANDO

Ay, and greater wonders than that.

ROSALIND

Oh, I know where you are. Nay, 'tis true. There was never
anything so sudden but the fight of two rams and Caesar's
thrasonical brag of "I came, saw, and overcame." For your
30   brother and my sister no sooner met but they looked, no
sooner looked but they loved, no sooner loved but they
sighed, no sooner sighed but they asked one another the
reason, no sooner knew the reason but they sought the
remedy; and in these degrees have they made a pair of stairs
35   to marriage, which they will climb incontinent, or else be
incontinent before marriage. They are in the very wrath of
love, and they will together. Clubs cannot part them.

ORLANDO

They shall be married tomorrow, and I will bid the duke to
the nuptial. But Oh, how bitter a thing it is to look into
40   happiness through another man's eyes. By so much the
more shall I tomorrow be at the height of heart-heaviness,
by how much I shall think my brother happy in having what
he wishes for.

ORLANDO

Actually, it's my arm.

ROSALIND

I thought your heart had been wounded by a lion's claws.

ORLANDO

My heart *has* been wounded, but by a lady, not a lion.

ROSALIND

Did your brother tell you how well I pretended to faint when he showed me the handkerchief?

ORLANDO

Yes, and he told me some things that were even more amazing.

ROSALIND

Oh, I know what you're talking about. It's true: it was as sudden as two rams rushing at each other, and as quick as Julius Caesar's "I came, I saw, I conquered." Your brother and my sister had no sooner met than they gave each other a good once over; they had no sooner looked at each other than they fell in love; no sooner fell in love than they sighed; no sooner sighed than they asked each other why they had sighed; no sooner answered than they sought a solution. And in this way, degree by degree, they've built a staircase toward marriage. And they had better climb those stairs immediately, or else they'll end up in bed before they ought to. They're in the heat of passion; they simply have to be together. You couldn't beat the two of them apart.

ORLANDO

They'll be married tomorrow, and I'll invite the duke to the ceremony. But, oh, it makes me bitter to look at happiness through another man's eyes. Tomorrow I'll be at the depths of my misery thinking about the happiness my brother has achieved, in having what he wished for.

ROSALIND
　　Why, then, tomorrow I cannot serve your turn for Rosalind?

ORLANDO
45　　I can live no longer by thinking.

ROSALIND
　　I will weary you then no longer with idle talking. Know of
　　me then—for now I speak to some purpose—that I know
　　you are a gentleman of good conceit. I speak not this that
　　you should bear a good opinion of my knowledge,
50　　insomuch I say I know you are. Neither do I labor for a
　　greater esteem than may in some little measure draw a
　　belief from you to do yourself good, and not to grace me.
　　Believe then, if you please, that I can do strange things. I
　　have, since I was three year old, conversed with a magician,
55　　most profound in his art and yet not damnable. If you do
　　love Rosalind so near the heart as your gesture cries it out,
　　when your brother marries Aliena shall you marry her. I
　　know into what straits of fortune she is driven, and it is not
　　impossible to me, if it appear not inconvenient to you, to set
60　　her before your eyes tomorrow, human as she is, and
　　without any danger.

ORLANDO
　　Speak'st thou in sober meanings?

ROSALIND
　　By my life I do, which I tender dearly, though I say I am a
　　magician. Therefore put you in your best array, bid your
65　　friends; for if you will be married tomorrow, you shall, and
　　to Rosalind, if you will.

　　Enter SILVIUS *and* PHOEBE

　　Look, here comes a lover of mine and a lover of hers.

PHOEBE
　　Youth, you have done me much ungentleness
　　To show the letter that I writ to you.

ROSALIND

Well then, can't I act as Rosalind for you tomorrow?

ORLANDO

I can't live by pretending anymore.

ROSALIND

I won't exhaust you anymore with idle chitchat. You should know that I think you're a smart man. I really mean it. I'm not telling you this so you'll think well of me (who wouldn't think well of someone who thought well of him, after all?) And I'm not trying to enhance my own reputation, but only to do you good. Believe me, then, that I have special powers. Since I was three years old, I've been in contact with a powerful but virtuous magician—no black magic here. If you love Rosalind as much as you say you do, you will marry her when your brother marries Aliena. I know where she is and, if you don't mind, I will set her before you tomorrow, whole and unharmed.

ORLANDO

Are you serious?

ROSALIND

I swear on my life, which I take pretty seriously, even if I am a magician. So put on your best clothes and tell your friends to come. Because if you want to be married tomorrow, you will, and if you want to be married to Rosalind, you will.

SILVIUS *and* PHOEBE *enter.*

Look, here comes someone who loves me, along with someone who loves her.

PHOEBE

Young man, it was very rude of you to show him the letter I wrote you.

ROSALIND

70   I care not if I have. It is my study
To seem despiteful and ungentle to you.
You are there followed by a faithful shepherd.
Look upon him, love him; he worships you.

PHOEBE

Good shepherd, tell this youth what 'tis to love.

SILVIUS

75   It is to be all made of sighs and tears,
And so am I for Phoebe.

PHOEBE

And I for Ganymede.

ORLANDO

And I for Rosalind.

ROSALIND

And I for no woman.

SILVIUS

80   It is to be all made of faith and service,
And so am I for Phoebe.

PHOEBE

And I for Ganymede.

ORLANDO

And I for Rosalind.

ROSALIND

And I for no woman.

SILVIUS

85   It is to be all made of fantasy,
All made of passion and all made of wishes,
All adoration, duty, and observance,
All humbleness, all patience and impatience,
All purity, all trial, all observance,

90   And so am I for Phoebe.

PHOEBE

And so am I for Ganymede.

ORLANDO

And so am I for Rosalind.

ROSALIND

I don't care. I'm being contemptuous and cruel toward you on purpose. A faithful shepherd worships you. Why don't you pay attention to him? Why don't you love him? He adores you.

PHOEBE

Silvius, tell this youth what it means to be in love.

SILVIUS

It means being full of sighs and tears, like I am for Phoebe.

PHOEBE

And like I am for Ganymede.

ORLANDO

And like I am for Rosalind.

ROSALIND

And like I am for no woman.

SILVIUS

It means being faithful and ready to serve, just like I am for Phoebe.

PHOEBE

And like I am for Ganymede.

ORLANDO

And like I am for Rosalind.

ROSALIND

And like I am for no woman.

SILVIUS

It means being filled with fantasy; with passion and wishes; with adoration, loyalty, and devotion. It means being humble, being patient, being impatient, being pure, being put-upon, being obedient. Just as I am for Phoebe.

PHOEBE

And I for Ganymede.

ORLANDO

And I for Rosalind.

ROSALIND

And so am I for no woman.

PHOEBE

If this be so, why blame you me to love you?

SILVIUS

95   If this be so, why blame you me to love you?

ORLANDO

If this be so, why blame you me to love you?

ROSALIND

Why do you speak, too, "Why blame you me to love you?"?

ORLANDO

To her that is not here, nor doth not hear.

ROSALIND

Pray you, no more of this. 'Tis like the howling of Irish
100   wolves against the moon. *(to* SILVIUS*)* I will help you, if I
can. *(to* PHOEBE*)* I would love you if I could.—Tomorrow
meet me all together. *(to* PHOEBE*)* I will marry you if ever I
marry woman, and I'll be married tomorrow. *(to* ORLANDO*)*
I will satisfy you if ever I satisfy man, and you shall be
105   married tomorrow. *(to* SILVIUS*)* I will content you, if what
pleases you contents you, and you shall be married
tomorrow. *(to* ORLANDO*)* As you love Rosalind, meet. *(to*
SILVIUS*)* As you love Phoebe, meet.—And as I love no
woman, I'll meet. So fare you well. I have left you
110   commands.

SILVIUS

I'll not fail, if I live.

PHOEBE

Nor I.

ORLANDO

Nor I.

Exeunt

ROSALIND

And I for no woman.

PHOEBE

Since you know all this is true, why do you blame me for loving you?

SILVIUS

And why do you blame me for loving you?

ORLANDO

And why do you blame me for loving you?

ROSALIND

Who are you talking to?

ORLANDO

I'm saying it to the girl who isn't here and doesn't hear me.

ROSALIND

All right, stop this. You sound like a pack of wolves howling at the moon. *(to* SILVIUS*)* I'll help you, if I can. *(to* PHOEBE*)* If I could love you, I would. All of you, meet me here tomorrow. *(to* PHOEBE*)* If I'm ever going to marry a woman, I'll marry you. And I *am* getting married tomorrow. *(to* ORLANDO*)* If I will ever satisfy a man, I'll satisfy you. And you will get married tomorrow. *(to* SILVIUS*)* If the thing you desire will make you happy, I'll make you happy. And you'll get married tomorrow. *(to* ORLANDO*)* By the love you have for Rosalind, come back tomorrow. *(to* SILVIUS*)* By the love you have for Phoebe, come here tomorrow.— And by my love for no woman, I'll also be here tomorrow. So, goodbye for now. You all know what to do.

SILVIUS

As long as I'm alive, I'll be here.

PHOEBE

Me too.

ORLANDO

Me too.

They all exit.

ACT 5, SCENE 3

Enter TOUCHSTONE *and* AUDREY.

TOUCHSTONE
Tomorrow is the joyful day, Audrey. Tomorrow will we be married.

AUDREY
I do desire it with all my heart, and I hope it is no dishonest desire to desire to be a woman of the world.

Enter two PAGES

5   Here comes two of the banished duke's pages.

FIRST PAGE
Well met, honest gentleman.

TOUCHSTONE
By my troth, well met. Come, sit, sit, and a song.

SECOND PAGE
We are for you. Sit i' th' middle.

FIRST PAGE
Shall we clap into 't roundly, without hawking or spitting or
10   saying we are hoarse, which are the only prologues to a bad voice?

SECOND PAGE
I' faith, i' faith, and both in a tune like two gypsies on a horse.

PAGES
(sing)
It was a lover and his lass,
15   *With a hey, and a ho, and a hey-nonny-no,*
That o'er the green cornfield did pass
In springtime, the only pretty ring time,
When birds do sing, Hey ding a ding, ding.
Sweet lovers love the spring.
20   *Between the acres of the rye,*

ACT 5, SCENE 3

TOUCHSTONE *and* AUDREY *enter.*

TOUCHSTONE

Tomorrow is the happy day, Audrey. We'll be married tomorrow.

AUDREY

I can't wait. I hope it doesn't make me unchaste that I really want to be a married woman. Here come two of Duke Senior's pages.

Two PAGES *enter.*

FIRST PAGE

Good afternoon, good gentleman.

TOUCHSTONE

It really is good to see you. Come, sit, sit, and sing me a song.

SECOND PAGE

Sounds good to us. Sit between us.

FIRST PAGE

Should we just get down to it? Should we skip all that hacking and spitting and saying that we're hoarse, which only makes clear what lousy singers we are?

SECOND PAGE

Yes, yes, and let's sing in unison, like two gypsies riding on a single horse.

PAGES

(singing)
There was a lover and his girl,
With a hey, and a ho, and a hey-nonny-no,
Who walked through the cornfield
In the springtime, the only proper wedding time,
The time when birds sing, Hey ding-a-ding-ding.
Sweet lovers love the spring.

With a hey, and a ho, and a hey-nonny-no,
These pretty country folks would lie
In springtime, the only pretty ring time,
When birds do sing, Hey ding a ding, ding.
25 *Sweet lovers love the spring.*
This carol they began that hour,
With a hey, and a ho, and a hey hey-nonny-no,
How that a life was but a flower
In springtime, the only pretty ring time,
30 *When birds do sing, Hey ding a ding, ding.*
Sweet lovers love the spring.
And therefore take the present time,
With a hey, and a ho, and a hey hey-nonny-no,
For love is crownèd with the prime
35 *In springtime, the only pretty ring time,*
When birds do sing, Hey ding a ding, ding.
Sweet lovers love the spring.

TOUCHSTONE
Truly, young gentlemen, though there was no great matter in the ditty, yet the note was very untunable.

FIRST PAGE
40 You are deceived, sir. We kept time. We lost not our time.

TOUCHSTONE
By my troth, yes. I count it but time lost to hear such a foolish song. God be wi' you, and God mend your voices.— Come, Audrey.

Exeunt

Between the acres of rye,
With a hey, and a ho, and a hey-nonny-no
The pretty country folk would lie
In the springtime, the only proper wedding-time,
The time when birds sing, Hey ding-a-ding-ding.
Sweet lovers love the spring.
They wrote this song at that time,
With a hey, and a ho, and a hey-nonny-no,
About how life was as short-lived as a flower
In the springtime, the only proper wedding time,
The time when birds sing, hey ding-a-ding-ding.
Sweet lovers love the spring.
So seize the present time,
With a hey, and a ho, and a hey-nonny-no,
For love is all perfection
In the springtime, the only proper wedding time,
The time when birds sing, Hey ding-a-ding-ding.
Sweet lovers love the spring.

TOUCHSTONE

Really, young men, though it wasn't a very hard song to get right, the music was still all out of tune.

FIRST PAGE

In other words, they kept the rhythm and didn't speed up. However, Touchstone was complaining not about the rhythm but about the melody.

No, sir, you're wrong; we kept the song's time, we didn't lose any.

TOUCHSTONE

Oh, yes you did—I lost time listening to your foolish song. God be with you, and I hope He fixes your voices! Come on, Audrey.

They all exit.

ACT 5, SCENE 4

Enter DUKE SENIOR, AMIENS, JAQUES, ORLANDO, OLIVER,
and CELIA

DUKE SENIOR
Dost thou believe, Orlando, that the boy
Can do all this that he hath promisèd?

ORLANDO
I sometimes do believe and sometimes do not,
As those that fear they hope, and know they fear.

Enter ROSALIND, SILVIUS, *and* PHOEBE

ROSALIND
5   *(as Ganymede)* Patience once more whiles our compact
          is urged.
       (to DUKE SENIOR*)* You say, if I bring in your Rosalind,
       You will bestow her on Orlando here?

DUKE SENIOR
       That would I, had I kingdoms to give with her.

ROSALIND
10   *(to* ORLANDO*)* And you say you will have her when I bring
       her?

ORLANDO
       That would I, were I of all kingdoms king.

ROSALIND
       (to PHOEBE*)* You say you'll marry me if I be willing?

PHOEBE
       That will I, should I die the hour after.

ROSALIND
15   But if you do refuse to marry me,
       You'll give yourself to this most faithful shepherd?

ACT 5, SCENE 4

DUKE SENIOR, AMIENS, JAQUES, ORLANDO, OLIVER,
and CELIA *enter.*

DUKE SENIOR

Orlando, do you really believe that this boy can do everything he's promised?

ORLANDO

Sometimes I do and sometimes I don't. I'm afraid of hoping, but I hope anyway.

ROSALIND, SILVIUS, *and* PHOEBE *enter.*

ROSALIND

(as Ganymede) Be patient for a bit longer while I go over the terms of our agreement. *(to* DUKE SENIOR*)* You say that if I bring Rosalind here, you will give her to Orlando in marriage?

DUKE SENIOR

Yes, even if I had whole kingdoms to give along with her.

ROSALIND

(to ORLANDO*)* And you promise to marry her, when I bring her here?

ORLANDO

I will, even if I were king of all kingdoms.

ROSALIND

(to PHOEBE*)* And you say you'll marry me, if I'm willing to marry you?

PHOEBE

Yes, even if I die an hour later.

ROSALIND

But if you decide not to marry me, you'll marry this faithful shepherd instead?

PHOEBE
> So is the bargain.

ROSALIND
> *(to* SILVIUS*)* You say that you'll have Phoebe if she will?

SILVIUS
> Though to have her and death were both one thing.

ROSALIND
20 > I have promised to make all this matter even.
> Keep you your word, O duke, to give your daughter,
> —You yours, Orlando, to receive his daughter.
> —Keep your word, Phoebe, that you'll marry me
> Or else, refusing me, to wed this shepherd.
25 > —Keep your word, Silvius, that you'll marry her
> If she refuse me. And from hence I go
> To make these doubts all even.

Exeunt ROSALIND *and* CELIA

DUKE SENIOR
> I do remember in this shepherd boy
> Some lively touches of my daughter's favor.

ORLANDO
30 > My lord, the first time that I ever saw him
> Methought he was a brother to your daughter.
> But, my good lord, this boy is forest-born
> And hath been tutored in the rudiments
> Of many desperate studies by his uncle,
35 > Whom he reports to be a great magician
> Obscurèd in the circle of this forest.

Enter TOUCHSTONE *and* AUDREY

PHOEBE

That's the deal.

ROSALIND

(to SILVIUS) And you agree to marry Phoebe, if she is willing?

SILVIUS

Even if marrying her meant I died.

ROSALIND

I've promised to make everything right. Duke Senior, keep your promise to give away your daughter. Orlando, keep your promise to marry his daughter. Phoebe, keep your promise to marry me, and to marry this shepherd if you choose to refuse me. Silvius, keep your promise to marry Phoebe if she refuses me. I'll leave now, to set all these things right.

ROSALIND and CELIA exit.

DUKE SENIOR

This shepherd boy reminds me quite vividly of my daughter.

ORLANDO

My lord, when I first saw him I thought he was your daughter's brother. But, my lord, this boy was born in the forest and has been schooled not in the usual subjects but only in magic. His uncle, who the boy says is a great magician and lives concealed within the boundaries of this forest, taught him.

TOUCHSTONE and AUDREY enter.

JAQUES
> There is sure another flood toward, and these couples are
> coming to the ark. Here comes a pair of very strange beasts,
> which in all tongues are called fools.

TOUCHSTONE
40 Salutation and greeting to you all.

JAQUES
> Good my lord, bid him welcome. This is the motley-
> minded gentleman that I have so often met in the forest. He
> hath been a courtier, he swears.

TOUCHSTONE
> If any man doubt that, let him put me to my purgation. I
45 have trod a measure. I have flattered a lady. I have been
> politic with my friend, smooth with mine enemy. I have
> undone three tailors. I have had four quarrels, and like to
> have fought one.

JAQUES
> And how was that ta'en up?

TOUCHSTONE
50 Faith, we met and found the quarrel was upon the seventh
> cause.

JAQUES
> How "seventh cause"?—Good my lord, like this fellow.

DUKE SENIOR
> I like him very well.

JAQUES

In the biblical story of Noah, God sends a flood to wash away mankind and tells Noah to take two of every animal on a ship, so that the world can be repopulated later. Touchstone and Audrey are the latest twosome in "Noah's ark" of marriages.

Well, look: there must be another flood coming, with these couples also on their way to Noah's ark. Here comes a pair of those strange creatures called "fools" in any language.

TOUCHSTONE

Hello, and greetings to you all.

JAQUES

My lord, welcome this man. This is the jester I have met so many times in the forest. He swears he used to be a courtier.

TOUCHSTONE

If anyone doubts this, let him put me on trial. I have danced a round, I have flattered a lady, I have been polite with my friends, smooth and cunning with my enemies. I have bankrupted three tailors. I have quarreled four times, and almost got in a fight.

JAQUES

And how was that one settled?

TOUCHSTONE

Well, we almost fought and then realized that we had reached the seventh cause.

JAQUES

What do you mean, the seventh cause? (to DUKE SENIOR) My good lord, I hope you like this fellow.

DUKE SENIOR

I like him very well.

TOUCHSTONE

God 'ild you, sir. I desire you of the like. I press in here, sir,
amongst the rest of the country copulatives, to swear and to
forswear, according as marriage binds and blood breaks. A
poor virgin, sir, an ill-favored thing, sir, but mine own. A
poor humor of mine, sir, to take that that no man else will.
Rich honesty dwells like a miser, sir, in a poor house, as
your pearl in your foul oyster.

DUKE SENIOR

By my faith, he is very swift and sententious.

TOUCHSTONE

According to the fool's bolt, sir, and such dulcet diseases.

JAQUES

But for the seventh cause. How did you find the quarrel on
the seventh cause?

TOUCHSTONE

Upon a lie seven times removed.—Bear your body more
seeming, Audrey.—As thus, sir: I did dislike the cut of a
certain courtier's beard. He sent me word if I said his beard
was not cut well, he was in the mind it was. This is called
"the retort courteous." If I sent him word again it was not
well cut, he would send me word he cut it to please himself.
This is called "the quip modest." If again it was not well
cut, he disabled my judgment. This is called "the reply
churlish." If again it was not well cut, he would answer I
spake not true. This is called "the reproof valiant." If again
it was not well cut, he would say I lie. This is called "the
countercheck quarrelsome," and so to "the lie
circumstantial" and "the lie direct."

JAQUES

And how oft did you say his beard was not well cut?

TOUCHSTONE

> God bless you, sir. I want the same thing as all these other people. I've come here to be married, like all these other would-be couples. This poor virgin isn't much to look at, sir, but she's mine. It's a strange habit of mine to take the thing that no one else wants: virginity in an ugly girl is like a rich man living in a broken-down house or a pearl in the hideous oyster.

DUKE SENIOR

> Really, he's very witty, and full of wise sayings.

TOUCHSTONE

> His wittiness, a sweet disease, is here one minute and gone the next, sir, as with most fools.

JAQUES

> But back to that argument you mentioned. What's the "seventh cause"?

TOUCHSTONE

> Our argument went through seven stages—watch your posture, Audrey.—It went like this. I didn't like the way a particular courtier had cut his beard. He sent me word that, whether I liked it or not, he liked it fine. They call this "the courteous retort." If I repeat that it isn't cut well, and he responds that he isn't trying to please me, just himself, with his beard. They call this "the modest quip." If I say again it is poorly cut, and he responds that my judgment is no good, they call this "the sullen reply." If I say yet again that his beard is poorly cut, and he says that I'm not speaking the truth, they call this "the brave retort." One more time I say it's not well cut, and he says I'm lying. They call this "the argumentative countercheck." And so on through "the circumstantial lie" and "the direct lie."

JAQUES

> And how many times did you say his beard wasn't cut well?

TOUCHSTONE
I durst go no further than the lie circumstantial, nor he
80   durst not give me the lie direct, and so we measured swords
and parted.

JAQUES
Can you nominate in order now the degrees of the lie?

TOUCHSTONE
O sir, we quarrel in print, by the book, as you have books for
good manners. I will name you the degrees: the first, "the
85   retort courteous"; the second, "the quip modest"; the
third, "the reply churlish"; the fourth, "the reproof
valiant"; the fifth, "the countercheque quarrelsome"; the
sixth, "the lie with circumstance"; the seventh, "the lie
direct." All these you may avoid but the lie direct, and you
90   may avoid that, too, with an "if." I knew when seven
justices could not take up a quarrel, but when the parties
were met themselves, one of them thought but of an "if,"
as: "If you said so, then I said so." And they shook hands
and swore brothers. Your "if" is the only peacemaker: much
95   virtue in "if."

JAQUES
Is not this a rare fellow, my lord? He's as good at anything
and yet a fool.

DUKE SENIOR
He uses his folly like a stalking-horse, and under the
presentation of that he shoots his wit.

Enter HYMEN, ROSALIND, *and* CELIA. *Soft music*

HYMEN
100   Then is there mirth in heaven
When earthly things, made even,
Atone together.

TOUCHSTONE

I didn't dare take it past "the circumstantial lie," and he didn't dare go to the "direct lie," so we compared the lengths of our swords and then ended the fight.

Before a duel, opponents usually compared the length of their swords.

JAQUES

Can you name the steps of that argument again?

TOUCHSTONE

Of course, sir. There are rulebooks for arguing just as there are rulebooks for manners. Here are the steps. First is "the courteous retort"; second, "the modest quip"; third, "the sullen reply"; fourth, "the valiant retort"; fifth, "the argumentative countercheck"; sixth, "the circumstantial lie"; seventh, "the direct lie." You can avoid getting to that final stage if you can properly use an "if." I once heard of an argument that seven judges couldn't settle. The two parties met up on their own, and one said, "Well, if you said this-and-that, then I must have said such-and-such," and they shook hands and parted on good terms. "If" is the only peacemaker. "If" is a very valuable word.

JAQUES

Isn't he a remarkable fellow, my lord? He's as smart as they come, but just a jester.

DUKE SENIOR

He uses his clownishness to disguise his deadly wit.

Hymen is the mythological god of marriage.

HYMEN *enters with* **ROSALIND** *and* **CELIA**, *dressed as themselves.*

Soft music plays.

HYMEN

There is laughter in heaven
When earthly affairs are put right
And people unite.

Good duke, receive thy daughter.
Hymen from heaven brought her,
105   Yea, brought her hither,
That thou mightst join her hand with his
Whose heart within his bosom is.

ROSALIND
(to **DUKE SENIOR***)* To you I give myself, for I am yours.
(to **ORLANDO***)* To you I give myself, for I am yours.

DUKE SENIOR
110   If there be truth in sight, you are my daughter.

ORLANDO
If there be truth in sight, you are my Rosalind.

PHOEBE
If sight and shape be true,
Why then, my love adieu.

ROSALIND
(to **DUKE SENIOR***)* I'll have no father, if you be not he.
115   *(to* **ORLANDO***)* I'll have no husband, if you be not he,
(to **PHOEBE***)* Nor ne'er wed woman, if you be not she.

HYMEN
Peace, ho! I bar confusion.
'Tis I must make conclusion
Of these most strange events.
120   Here's eight that must take hands
To join in Hymen's bands,
If truth holds true contents.
(to **ORLANDO** *and* **ROSALIND***)* You and you no cross shall part.
(to **OLIVER** *and* **CELIA***)* You and you are heart in heart.
125   *(to* **PHOEBE***)* You to his love must accord
Or have a woman to your lord.
(to **TOUCHSTONE** *and* **AUDREY***)* You and you are sure together
As the winter to foul weather.
(to all) Whiles a wedlock hymn we sing,
130   Feed yourselves with questioning,
That reason wonder may diminish
How thus we met, and these things finish.

Good duke, come receive your daughter.
Hymen brought her from heaven
Yes, brought her here.

ROSALIND

(to DUKE SENIOR*)* I give myself to you, for I am yours.
(to ORLANDO*)* I give myself to you, for I am yours.

DUKE SENIOR

If my eyes don't deceive me, you are my daughter.

ORLANDO

If my eyes don't deceive me, you are my Rosalind.

PHOEBE

If my eyes aren't deceiving me, goodbye, love.

ROSALIND

(to DUKE SENIOR*)* If you won't be my father, I won't
have any.
(to ORLANDO*)* If you won't be my husband, I won't
have any.
(to PHOEBE*)* If you won't be my wife, I won't have any.

HYMEN

Quiet! Stop chattering until I've made everything
clear. There are eight people here that I will join in
marriage, if the truth you see before you pleases you.
(to ORLANDO *and* ROSALIND*)* No hardship can part
you. *(to* OLIVER *and* CELIA*)* Your hearts are together.
(to PHOEBE*)* You must consent to having Silvius as your
husband, unless you'd rather be married to a woman.
(to TOUCHSTONE *and* AUDREY*)* You are bound to each
other as closely as winter is to bad weather. *(to all the
married couples)* While we sing a wedding hymn, satisfy your curiosity with questioning. Your surprise
will fade, and you'll learn how all this came to be.

(sings)
Wedding is great Juno's crown,
O blessèd bond of board and bed.
135 *'Tis Hymen peoples every town.*
High wedlock then be honorèd.
Honor, high honor, and renown,
To Hymen, god of every town.

DUKE SENIOR
O my dear niece, welcome thou art to me,
140 Even daughter, welcome in no less degree.

PHOEBE
I will not eat my word. Now thou art mine,
Thy faith my fancy to thee doth combine.

Enter JAQUES DE BOYS

JAQUES DE BOYS
Let me have audience for a word or two.
I am the second son of old Sir Rowland,
145 That bring these tidings to this fair assembly.
Duke Frederick, hearing how that every day
Men of great worth resorted to this forest,
Addressed a mighty power, which were on foot
In his own conduct, purposely to take
150 His brother here and put him to the sword.
And to the skirts of this wild wood he came,
Where, meeting with an old religious man,
After some question with him, was converted
Both from his enterprise and from the world,
155 His crown bequeathing to his banished brother,
And all their lands restored to them again
That were with him exiled. This to be true
I do engage my life.

(singing)

> Juno was the Roman goddess of marriage.

Marriage is the crown Juno wears,
It's a holy bond of domesticity.
It's marriage that populates each town,
So marriage should be honored.
Honor, honor, and fame
Is due to Hymen, the god of every town.

DUKE SENIOR

My niece, you are welcome here as if you were my own daughter.

PHOEBE

(to SILVIUS*)* I won't go back on my promise; I'll marry you. You've won me over with your faith.

JAQUES DE BOYS enters.

JAQUES DE BOYS

Let me have your attention for a moment. I'm Sir Rowland's middle son, and I bring you news. When Duke Frederick heard that great, worthy men were coming to this forest every day, he raised a large army to invade this land and fight his brother. But just at the edge of the forest, he met an old religious man. He spoke with him for a while and decided not only to abandon his pursuit of his brother but even to retreat from the world. He's giving the throne to his banished brother and restoring all the men he'd exiled to their rightful lands. I swear on my life that I'm speaking the truth.

DUKE SENIOR
Welcome, young man.

160   Thou offer'st fairly to thy brothers' wedding:
To one his lands withheld, and to the other
A land itself at large, a potent dukedom.
—First, in this forest let us do those ends
That here were well begun and well begot,

165   And, after, every of this happy number
That have endured shrewd days and nights with us
Shall share the good of our returnèd fortune
According to the measure of their states.
Meantime, forget this new-fall'n dignity,

170   And fall into our rustic revelry.
—Play, music.—And you brides and bridegrooms all,
With measure heaped in joy to th' measures fall.

JAQUES
Sir, by your patience: if I heard you rightly,
The duke hath put on a religious life

175   And thrown into neglect the pompous court.

JAQUES DE BOYS
He hath.

JAQUES
To him will I. Out of these convertites
There is much matter to be heard and learned.
(*to* DUKE SENIOR)
You to your former honor I bequeath;

180   Your patience and your virtue well deserves it.
(*to* ORLANDO)
You to a love that your true faith doth merit.
(*to* OLIVER)
You to your land, and love, and great allies.
(*to* SILVIUS)
You to a long and well-deservèd bed.

DUKE SENIOR

> Welcome, young man: you bring a great present to your brothers' wedding. To Oliver, you return his lands; to Orlando, you give a whole dukedom, since he will inherit my land. But first, let's finish the things we started out here. Then I'll share the abundance of my returned fortune with all those that have stayed out here with me, according to the rank and status each of you enjoy. But until then, let's forget our nobility and enjoy some fun. Music, please. Brides and bridegrooms, dance your happiness away.

JAQUES

> Wait a minute, sir. Do you mean to say that the duke has abandoned the glamorous court to live as a monk?

JAQUES DE BOYS

> Yes, he has.

JAQUES

> I will go find him. There is much to be learned from these converts. *(to DUKE SENIOR)* I bestow on you your former honor, for your patience and virtue. *(to ORLANDO)* I give you the love that your faithfulness deserves *(to OLIVER)* and you your land, your love, and your great allies. *(to SILVIUS)* You get a long and well-deserved stay in bed, with your new wife.

(to TOUCHSTONE*)*
And you to wrangling, for thy loving voyage
185   Is but for two months victualled.—So to your pleasures.
I am for other than for dancing measures.

DUKE SENIOR
Stay, Jaques, stay.

JAQUES
To see no pastime I. What you would have
I'll stay to know at your abandoned cave.

Exit

DUKE SENIOR
190   Proceed, proceed. We'll so begin these rites
As we do trust they'll end, in true delights.

Dance

Exeunt all but ROSALIND

(to TOUCHSTONE*)* And you I expect to be up fighting soon. The honeymoon will last two months, tops.— And with that, you may all return to your dancing. I'm bound for another fate.

DUKE SENIOR

Stay, Jaques, stay here for a bit.

JAQUES

No, this fun is not for me. I'll wait for you in your cave, where you can tell me what you need from me.

He exits.

DUKE SENIOR

Let's proceed. We'll begin the ceremony the way we hope it will end—with delight.

Everyone dances.

Everyone exits except ROSALIND.

EPILOGUE

ROSALIND
    It is not the fashion to see the lady the epilogue, but it is no
more unhandsome than to see the lord the prologue. If it be
true that good wine needs no bush, 'tis true that a good play
needs no epilogue. Yet to good wine they do use good
bushes, and good plays prove the better by the help of good
epilogues. What a case am I in, then, that am neither a good
epilogue nor cannot insinuate with you in the behalf of a
good play. I am not furnished like a beggar; therefore to beg
will not become me. My way is to conjure you, and I'll
begin with the women. I charge you, O women, for the love
you bear to men, to like as much of this play as please you.
And I charge you, O men, for the love you bear to women—
as I perceive by your simpering, none of you hates them—
that between you and the women the play may please. If I
were a woman, I would kiss as many of you as had beards
that pleased me, complexions that liked me, and breaths
that I defied not. And I am sure as many as have good
beards, or good faces, or sweet breaths will, for my kind
offer, when I make curtsy, bid me farewell.

Exit

EPILOGUE

ROSALIND

You don't usually see a woman deliver an epilogue, but it's no worse than seeing a man deliver the pro-logue. If it's true that you don't need ivy to sell good wine, then it should also be true that a good play doesn't need an epilogue. But they use good-quality ivy to sell good wine, and a good play is improved by a good epilogue. But then I'm in a strange position, as I not only do not have a good epilogue, I'm not sure this was a good play. I'm not dressed like a beggar, so it wouldn't be becoming for me to beg. No, instead I'll bewitch you, and I'll start with the women. Women, in the name of the love you have for men, I demand that you like as much of this play as you feel like. Men, in the name of the women you love—and I can guess by your goofy smiles that none of you exactly hates them—the play will act as a nice toy for you and the ladies to share. If I actually were a woman, I'd kiss all of you that have beards that pleased me, complexions that I liked, and breath that wasn't foul. And I'm sure that all of you with nice beards, good faces, and sweet breath will, when I curtsy good night, give me a nice round of applause.

She exits.

> Branches of ivy were hung in tavern windows to advertise the wine.

> In Shakespeare's day, boys played all the women's parts.

SPARKNOTES LITERATURE GUIDES